D1537381

H E A T H
MIDDLE LEVEL
LITERATURE

Becoming Myself

We all have hidden strengths and talents. Finding them is an
accomplishment in itself. In what ways do you shine?

A U T H O R S

Donna Alvermann
Linda Miller Cleary
Kenneth Donelson
Donald Gallo
Alice Haskins
J. Howard Johnston
John Lounsbury
Alleen Pace Nilsen
Robert Pavlik
Jewell Parker Rhodes
Alberto Alvaro Ríos
Sandra Schurr
Lyndon Searfoss
Julia Thomason
Max Thompson
Carl Zon

D.C. Heath and Company
Lexington, Massachusetts / Toronto, Ontario

STAFF CREDITS

EDITORIAL Barbara A. Brennan, Helen Byers, Christopher Johnson, Kathleen Kennedy Kelley, Owen Shows, Rita M. Sullivan
Proofreading: JoAnne B. Sgroi

CONTRIBUTING WRITERS Nance Davidson, Florence Harris

SERIES DESIGN Robin Herr

BOOK DESIGN Caroline Bowden, Daniel Derdula, Susan Geer, Diana Maloney, Angela Sciaraffa, Bonnie Chayes Yousefian
Art Editing: Carolyn Langley

PHOTOGRAPHY *Series Photography Coordinator:* Carmen Johnson
Photo Research Supervisor: Martha Friedman
Photo Researchers: Wendy Enright, Linda Finigan, Po-yee McKenna, PhotoSearch, Inc., Gillian Speeth, Denise Theodores
Assignment Photography Coordinators: Susan Doheny, Gayna Hoffman, Shawna Johnston

COMPUTER PREPRESS Ricki Pappo, Kathy Meisl
Richard Curran, Michele Locatelli

PERMISSIONS Dorothy B. McLeod

PRODUCTION Patrick Connolly

Cover Photograph: © Myron J. Dorf, The Stock Market. **Cover Design:** Robin Herr

Published simultaneously in Canada

Printed in the United States of America

International Standard Book Number: 0-669-32105-2 (soft cover); 0-669-38174-8 (hard cover)
2 3 4 5 6 7 8 9 10-RRD-99 98 97 96 95 94

Middle Level Authors

Donna Alvermann, University of Georgia
Alice Haskins, Howard County Public Schools, Maryland
J. Howard Johnston, University of South Florida
John Lounsbury, Georgia College
Sandra Schurr, University of South Florida
Julia Thomason, Appalachian State University
Max Thompson, Appalachian State University
Carl Zon, California Assessment Collaborative

Literature and Language Arts Authors

Linda Miller Cleary, University of Minnesota
Kenneth Donelson, Arizona State University
Donald Gallo, Central Connecticut State University
Alleen Pace Nilsen, Arizona State University
Robert Pavlik, Cardinal Stritch College, Milwaukee
Jewell Parker Rhodes, Arizona State University
Alberto Alvaro Ríos, Arizona State University
Lyndon Searfoss, Arizona State University

Teacher Consultants

Suzanne Aubin, Patapsco Middle School, Ellicott City, Maryland
Judy Baxter, Newport News Public Schools, Newport News, Virginia
Saundra Bryn, Director of Research and Development, El Mirage, Arizona
Lorraine Gerhart, Elmbrook Middle School, Elm Grove, Wisconsin
Kathy Tuchman Glass, Burlingame Intermediate School, Burlingame, California
Lisa Mandelbaum, Crocker Middle School, Hillsborough, California
Lucretia Pannozzo, John Jay Middle School, Katonah, New York
Carol Schultz, Jerling Junior High, Orland Park, Illinois
Jeanne Siebenman, Grand Canyon University, Phoenix, Arizona
Gail Thompson, Garey High School, Pomona, California
Rufus Thompson, Grace Yokley School, Ontario, California
Tom Tufts, Conniston Middle School, West Palm Beach, Florida
Edna Turner, Harpers Choice Middle School, Columbia, Maryland
C. Anne Webb, Buerkle Junior High School, St. Louis, Missouri
Geri Yaccino, Thompson Junior High School, St. Charles, Illinois

CONTENTS

Cornfield with Cypresses Vincent van Gogh. National Gallery, London

ASKING BIG QUESTIONS ABOUT THE LITERATURE

PROJECTS

1 WRITING WORKSHOP

DESCRIBING A HEROIC ACT   106-111

Write an eyewitness report describing an event in which an ordinary person became a hero.

2 COOPERATIVE LEARNING

A TIME CAPSULE   112-113

Create a time capsule of information about yourself and your world.

3 HELPING YOUR COMMUNITY

BECOME AN INSPIRATION   114-115

Express your unique creativity in artwork that will inspire others to see and appreciate their own special qualities.

Give Yourself a Hand

Who are you? Silly question, right? You're Sally Ling or Andrew Doyle or María Elena Ortíz or . . . whatever your name may be. You're X years old and a Yth grader at Z School.

But those details don't tell much—if anything—about you; they're just statistics. You, whoever you are, have a certain chin and talents and background and feelings. You're a complicated mixture, and you can't be labeled so easily.

So who are you really? Start figuring that out by giving yourself a hand—two hands, in fact—for all the things that are special about you.

1 A handsome list.

Look around you. What are the special characteristics of the people you see? Certain things are obvious, of course. Some wear glasses, are tall or short, have red hair or black hair. Some are terrific at basketball or math or art. But people have special qualities that aren't always obvious, too. Some are helpful to others or can keep a secret. Others are great puzzle-solvers. Some learn new languages easily or can dance. Others are natural leaders, or good sports, or good at fixing things.

With the whole class, brainstorm a long list of positive qualities people can have. Write the list in your journal.

Hand it to yourself.

Working alone, go over the list of qualities. Which ones could also describe you? Don't worry about seeming conceited. Be good to yourself, and be honest. For example, have you ever helped people with their homework? Then you can be helpful. Are you good at putting colors together in your clothes? Then you're creative as well as colorful. Put a check mark beside every quality that applies to you. Then, in your journal, copy the word for each quality into a second list. Entitle this list "My Special Qualities."

Now stretch the second list. Yes, there are more good things about you! Think of these qualities and add them too.

Hands down.

Spread one of your hands, palm down, on a piece of paper. (Leave room for the other hand.) Carefully trace it, going around each finger. Now put the other hand palm down and trace it. Go over your own list of special qualities and choose ten qualities that describe you most. Write one in each finger of the hands you traced.

Finally write your name on one palm. On the other, draw an item you think represents you—such as a basketball, a musical note, or a smile.

Hands up!

When you're satisfied, hand your hands to a partner. What does your partner think? Is he or she surprised by something you included—or left out?

Finally link your paper hands with those of your classmates in a classroom display that shows everyone's strengths, abilities, and special qualities.

Asking Big Questions About the Theme

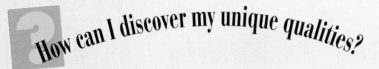

How can I discover my unique qualities?

List your unique qualities in one column of a chart like the one here. Next to each quality, write the name of an object the quality could also describe.

Choose the pair of words you like best and use them to finish the following sentence.

I am _____ than a _____. Are you *sharper* than a *pencil*? Or *brighter* than a *light bulb?*

Use the sentence in a shape poem in which the words form a picture of something in the poem.

Quality	Items
sharp	pencil
bright	light bulb

How can I improve my unique qualities?

Divide a sheet of paper into seven columns. Then label each column with the name of one of the following abilities.

Physical — Moving, acting out, playing
Social — Interacting with others
Personal — Understanding thoughts and feelings
Logical — Reasoning, problem solving
Musical — Making music, using rhythm
Verbal — Using language
Visual — Noticing shapes, creating art

Under each heading describe examples of how you have used that ability. Write a New Year's resolution telling which abilities you'd like to improve.

How can I share my unique qualities?

With a partner, think of ways to fill the blanks in the sentence "When I need help with _____, I call someone who's _____." Write them in your journal. Which qualities in the second blank also describe you? Circle them.

Draw an old-fashioned telephone like the one here. Write your name on the dial. Around it write five qualities—such as *creative* or *wise*—that tell why someone might call *you* for help.

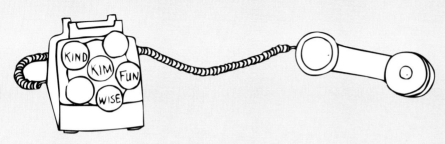

How does the world affect my unique qualities?

What places, people, activities, or things have influenced who you are? Maybe your aunt is a great storyteller, or once you went to a soccer camp, or you've lived in a foreign country. How was each ability listed on page 10 strengthened by that experience?

Design a postcard by drawing the place, activity, thing, or person who influenced you. On the back, explain to someone how your experience sparked one or more of your special qualities.

NOW
Think!

What are other questions you might ask about the qualities that make you unique? Make a list for yourself in your journal. In your reading, activities, and projects for *Becoming Myself*, think about these questions as well as the four Big Questions. Notice the ways that you uniquely answer them!

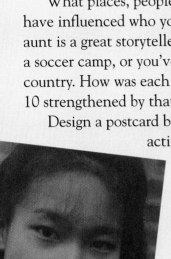

THE SUN AND THE MOON

BECOMING MYSELF

E L A I N E   L A R O N

The Sun is filled with shining light
It blazes far and wide
The Moon reflects the sunlight back
But has no light inside.

I think I'd rather be the Sun
That shines so bold and bright
Than be the Moon, that only glows
With someone else's light.

Who Am I?

STELLA MANCILLAS

I walk through crowded streets

Dirt and broken glass beneath my feet.

I gaze up at the crying red sky

And ask, "Who am I?"

Natural Answer Helen Frankenthaler, 1976, acrylic on canvas, 8' x 11', Art Gallery of Ontario, Toronto

JOYCE HOVELSRUD

YOUNG LADIES DON'T SLAY DRAGONS

A dragon with exceedingly evil intentions was plaguing[1] the Palace of Hexagon. Night and day he lurked about the courtyard walls, belching fire and smoke and roaring in a most terrible fashion. Things looked bad for the royal household.

"Mercy," said the queen.

"Dear me," said the king. "One of these days he'll get a royal blaze going, and when he does—poof! That'll be it."

"Well, what are you going to do about it?" asked the queen sharply. "I mean, you can't just sit there counting out your money and ignoring the problem."

"I have asked every brave man in the kingdom to slay the dragon," said the king. "They all said they had more important things to do."

"Nonsense," said the queen with a breathy sigh. "What could be more important than saving the palace from a monstrous dragon? Perhaps you should offer a reward."

"I *have* offered a reward," said the king. "No one seems interested."

"Well then, offer something of value to go with it," said the queen. And with that, she slammed the honey jar on the table and stomped out of the room.

"I'll slay the dragon," said the Princess Penelope, jumping from behind an antique suit of armor. There, she had just happened to be listening to the conversation while oiling a rusty joint.

The king blinked his eyes twice—once with shock because he was taken by surprise, and once with pride because he was taken by his daughter's dazzling beauty. "You can't

1. **plaguing** [plāg′ ing]: tormenting, troubling.

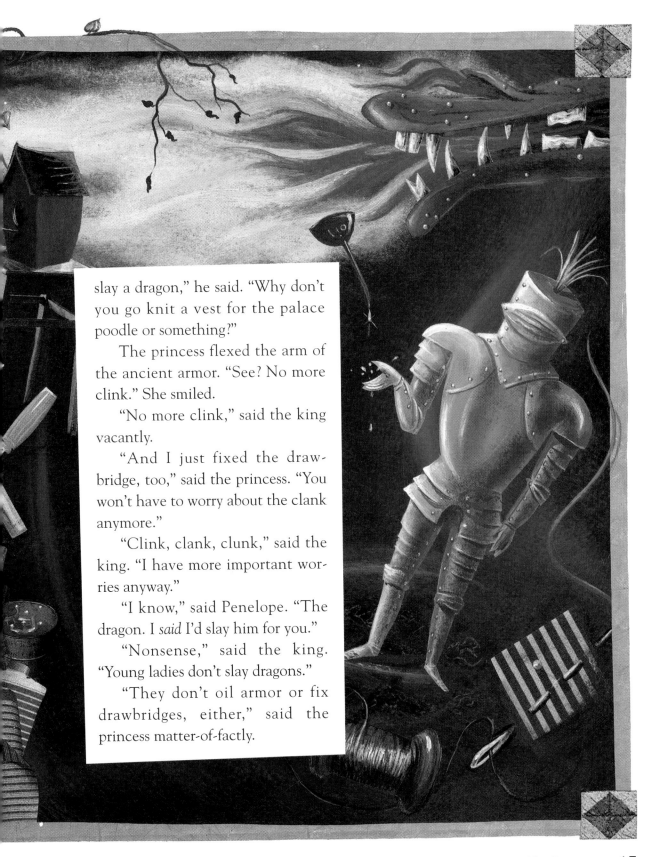

slay a dragon," he said. "Why don't you go knit a vest for the palace poodle or something?"

The princess flexed the arm of the ancient armor. "See? No more clink." She smiled.

"No more clink," said the king vacantly.

"And I just fixed the drawbridge, too," said the princess. "You won't have to worry about the clank anymore."

"Clink, clank, clunk," said the king. "I have more important worries anyway."

"I know," said Penelope. "The dragon. I *said* I'd slay him for you."

"Nonsense," said the king. "Young ladies don't slay dragons."

"They don't oil armor or fix drawbridges, either," said the princess matter-of-factly.

The king scratched his head and thought about that for a while. Princess Penelope was always giving him something to think about. For one thing, he thought her rare beauty was unsurpassed[2] by that of any princess on earth. For another, it seemed she never behaved as beautiful princesses should.

"Slaying dragons is men's work," he said finally, "and that's that."

The princess didn't really think that was that. But she knew her father did. So she said no more about it—to him, anyway.

It seemed to her that a young lady could do anything she wanted, if she set her mind to it. And in her tender years she had set her mind to many things the king and queen had said only men could do.

She once whittled[3] a whistle from a green willow stick when she was supposed to be sewing a fine seam.

She once built a birdhouse for the palace puffin[4] when she was supposed to be practicing her lute[5] lesson.

And once she even killed a mouse. She had come into the bedchamber to find her mother standing on a chair and screaming— as queens do in the presence of mice. "Don't worry, Mother, I'll get him," Penelope said.

"Young ladies don't kill mice," the queen said. "For heaven's sake, stand on a chair and scream along with me."

But Penelope didn't stand on a chair and scream. She caught the mouse and disposed of it tidily.

Well, she would dispose of the dragon, too. And she would get some ideas on how to go about it.

She went to speak to the royal cook. "How would you slay a dragon?" she asked.

"I would cut off his head with a carving knife," said the cook. "But of course you couldn't do that."

"Why not?" asked the princess.

"Young ladies don't slay dragons," the cook said.

"My father said that, too," said Penelope, and she went to speak to the royal tailor. "How would you slay a dragon?" she asked.

"I would stab him through the heart with a long needle," the tailor said.

2. **unsurpassed** [un′ sər pasd′]: not equaled.
3. **whittled** [hwit′ ld]: carved.
4. **puffin** [puf′ ən]: a sea bird with a thick body, a large head, and a bill of several colors.
5. **lute** [lüt]: a musical instrument, similar to a guitar, used in the 1500s and 1600s.

"Would you lend me a long needle?" asked the princess.

"Young ladies don't slay dragons," the tailor said. "Besides, I don't have a needle long enough or strong enough."

So Princess Penelope went to the royal court jester.[6] "How would you slay a dragon?" she asked.

"I would tell him such a funny story he would die laughing," said the jester.

"Do you have such a funny story?" asked Penelope.

"There aren't any stories *that* funny," said the jester. "Besides, young ladies don't slay dragons."

"You may be in for a surprise," said the princess, and she went to speak to the royal wizard. "How would you slay a dragon?" she asked.

The royal wizard thought a long time. Then he said, "Why do you want to know?"

"Because I want to slay the dragon," Penelope said matter-of-factly.

"Well, if you really want the truth," the wizard said, "the fact is, young ladies don't slay dragons."

"How do you know they don't?" Penelope asked.

"Everybody knows that," the wizard said. "Don't ask me how I know—it's just a fact."

"Well, then," the princess said, "if a brave young man wanted to save the palace from a smoke-blowing, flame-throwing, fierce and wicked dragon, what advice would you give him?"

The royal wizard wrinkled his forehead, squinted his eyes, and made arches with his fingers while he thought. Then he said, "I would advise him to fight fire with fire."

"I see," said Penelope.

"My feet are cold," said the wizard. "Do me a favor and slide that hot bucket over here. I want to warm my toes on it."

Penelope did as he bade. "How does the bucket stay hot?" she asked.

"It's filled with a magic liquid that burns without fire," said the wizard. "I conjured[7] it up myself."

"A good bit of magic," said Penelope admiringly. "Can you get the liquid to flame up?"

"If I want flames, I just drop a hot coal into the bucket," said the wizard. And then he fell asleep. He always fell asleep after talking three minutes, and now his three minutes were up. Besides, it was nap time for everybody in the palace.

---

6. **jester** [jes′ tər]: a man who told amusing stories to kings and their guests.

7. **conjured** [kon′ jərd]: caused to appear by using magic.

But how anybody could sleep through the dragon's terrible roaring was a mystery to Penelope. And how anybody could sleep while evil threatened the palace was another mystery to her.

The wizard had given the princess an idea, though, and she tiptoed out of the room.

She found a pipe in her collection of iron and sealed it at one end. She tiptoed back to the wizard's room and filled the pipe with liquid from the magic bucket. With a pair of tongs, she took a hot coal from the fire and tiptoed away. She paused in the great hall long enough to don a suit of armor—minus the helmet that hurt her ears and hung low over her eyes. Finally she found a shield she could lift.

Then, clanking, she made her way through the courtyard to the gates. Though she was not strong enough to open them, she managed to push herself sideways through the iron bars. And she wasn't the least bit afraid.

Now, the dragon was the biggest, the most ferocious dragon that ever lived. Princess Penelope didn't know that, but she rather suspected it, for why else wouldn't the brave men in the kingdom come to slay him?

And the dragon, who was also the wisest dragon that ever lived, had a hunch someone was after him. So he crept slowly around the walls to see who it was—roaring terrible roars and belching the sky full of fire and smoke as he went.

"I wish he wouldn't smoke so much," Penelope muttered as she crept after him. Rounding the corner, she could just make out the monstrous tip of the dragon's tail disappearing around the corner ahead.

"This will never do," she said after the third corner. Turning, she crept the other way—and she met the dragon face to face!

Now, it isn't easy to describe the ferocious battle that ensued, but it went something like this.

"Stop or I'll shoot," said Penelope calmly.

"What's a nice girl like you doing out slaying dragons?" sneered the dragon as he crept toward her, blinking several times because of her dazzling beauty.

"I said, stop or I'll shoot."

"You don't *shoot* dragons," the dragon said, coming closer. "Everybody I ever heard of slays them with swords."

"I'm not like everybody you ever heard of," Penelope said.

"I wonder why that is," the dragon said. And though he didn't know it at the time, the dragon had spoken his last words.

Princess Penelope raised her lead pipe, ignited the liquid with her hot coal, and dealt the deadly dragon a deadly blow.

Now, nobody would believe the terrible fire that followed, so it isn't necessary to describe it. But it was like the end of the world.

At last the smoke cleared away. And there, standing among the charred remains of the world's most ferocious dragon was—the world's most handsome prince. Penelope couldn't believe her eyes.

"I've been waiting for something like that to happen," said the prince, smiling a handsome smile and blinking a winsome[8] blink. "You'll marry me, of course."

8. **winsome** [win′ səm]: charming, pleasing.

But—Penelope was the world's most beautiful princess. Having her for a wife was more than the prince had dared dream, especially while bouncing about in the body of a dragon.

"I have a kingdom ten times the size of this pea patch," he added, "and it's all yours if you'll say yes."

Penelope gazed into his eyes a long time. Thoughtfully, she said, "I've been waiting for someone like you to ask me something like that. But there's something you should know about me first. I wouldn't be happy just being a queen and doing queen-things. I like to fix draw-bridges, build birdhouses, slay drag-ons—that sort of thing."

"It so happens I have bridges, birds, and dragons to spare," said the prince hopefully.

"Then my answer is yes," said Penelope.

And with that they saddled up a white horse and rode off into the sunset.

Now, even though this is the end of the story, you realize, of course, they are still living happily ever after.

MAYA ANGELOU

FROM

I KNOW WHY THE CAGED BIRD SINGS

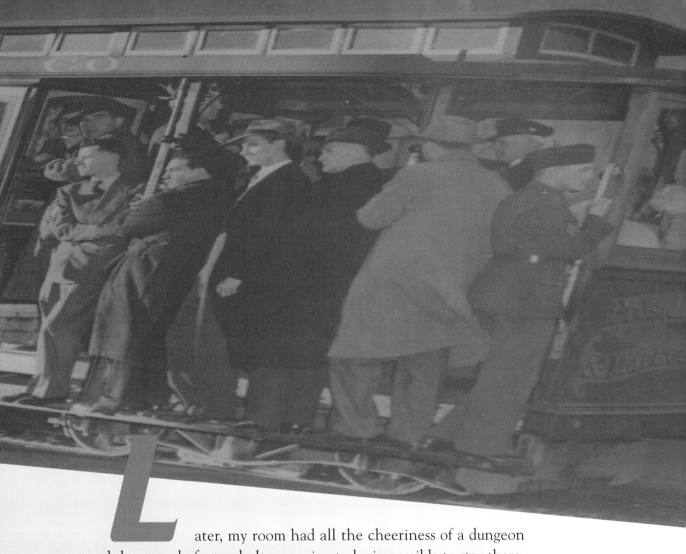

Later, my room had all the cheeriness of a dungeon and the appeal of a tomb. It was going to be impossible to stay there, but leaving held no attraction for me, either. Running away from home would be anticlimactic after Mexico, and a dull story after my month in the car lot. But the need for change bulldozed a road down the center of my mind.

I had it. The answer came to me with the suddenness of a collision. I would go to work. Mother wouldn't be difficult to convince; after all, in school I was a year ahead of my grade and Mother was a firm believer in self-sufficiency.[1] In fact, she'd be pleased to think that I had that much gumption,[2] that much of her in my character. (She liked to speak of herself as the original "do-it-yourself girl.")

1. **self-sufficiency** [self′ sə fish′ ən sē]: ability to take care of one's own needs.
2. **gumption** [gump′ shən]: fearlessness, energy.

Once I had settled on getting a job, all that remained was to decide which kind of job I was most fitted for. My intellectual pride had kept me from selecting typing, shorthand or filing as subjects in school, so office work was ruled out. War plants and shipyards demanded birth certificates, and mine would reveal me to be fifteen, and ineligible for work. So the well-paying defense jobs were also out. Women had replaced men on the streetcars as conductors and motormen, and the thought of sailing up and down the hills of San Francisco in a dark-blue uniform, with a money changer at my belt, caught my fancy.

Mother was as easy as I had anticipated. The world was moving so fast, so much money was being made, so many people were dying in Guam[3] and Germany, that hordes of strangers became good friends overnight. Life was cheap and death entirely free. How could she have the time to think about my academic career?

To her question of what I planned to do, I replied that I would get a job on the streetcars. She rejected the proposal with: "They don't accept colored people on the streetcars."

I would like to claim an immediate fury which was followed by the noble determination to break the restricting tradition. But the truth is, my first reaction was one of disappointment. I'd pictured myself, dressed in a neat blue serge suit, my money changer swinging jauntily[4] at my waist, and a cheery smile for the passengers which would make their own work day brighter.

From disappointment, I gradually ascended the emotional ladder to haughty[5] indignation, and finally to that state of stubbornness where the mind is locked like the jaws of an enraged bulldog.

I would go to work on the streetcars and wear a blue serge suit. Mother gave me her support with one of her usual terse[6] asides, "That's what you want to do? Then nothing beats a trial but a failure.

---

3. **Guam** [gwäm]: island and important U.S. military base in the western Pacific Ocean, east of the Philippines, which was heavily attacked during World War II.
4. **jauntily** [jôn′ tə lē]: in a carefree way.
5. **haughty** [hô′ tē]: too proud, scornful of others.
6. **terse** [tèrs]: brief and to the point.

Give it everything you've got. I've told you many times, 'Can't do is like Don't Care.' Neither of them have a home."

Translated, that meant there was nothing a person can't do, and there should be nothing a human being didn't care about. It was the most positive encouragement I could have hoped for.

In the offices of the Market Street Railway Company, the receptionist seemed as surprised to see me there as I was surprised to find the interior dingy and the décor drab. Somehow I had expected waxed surfaces and carpeted floors. If I had met no resistance, I might have decided against working for such a poor-mouth-looking concern. As it was, I explained that I had come to see about a job. She asked, was I sent by an agency, and when I replied that I was not, she told me they were only accepting applicants from agencies.

The classified pages of the morning papers had listed advertisements for motorettes and conductorettes and I reminded her of that. She gave me a face full of astonishment that my suspicious nature would not accept.

"I am applying for the job listed in this morning's *Chronicle* and I'd like to be presented to your personnel manager." While I spoke in supercilious[7] accents, and looked at the room as if I had an oil well in my own backyard, my armpits were being pricked by millions of hot pointed needles. She saw her escape and dived into it.

"He's out. He's out for the day. You might call tomorrow and if he's in, I'm sure you can see him." Then she swiveled her chair around on its rusty screws and with that I was supposed to be dismissed.

"May I ask his name?"

She half turned, acting surprised to find me still there.

"His name? Whose name?"

"Your personnel manager."

We were firmly joined in the hypocrisy[8] to play out the scene.

"The personnel manager? Oh, he's Mr. Cooper, but I'm not sure

7. **supercilious** [sü′ pər sil′ ē əs]: proud and filled with contempt for others.
8. **hypocrisy** [hi pok′ rə sē]: state of pretending to be good and polite.

you'll find him here tomorrow. He's . . . Oh, but you can try."

"Thank you."

"You're welcome."

And I was out of the musty room and into the even mustier lobby. In the street I saw the receptionist and myself going faithfully through paces that were stale with familiarity, although I had never encountered that kind of situation before and, probably, neither had she. We were like actors who, knowing the play by heart, were still able to cry afresh over the old tragedies and laugh spontaneously at the comic situations.

The miserable little encounter had nothing to do with me, the me of me, any more than it had to do with that silly clerk. The incident was a recurring dream, concocted[9] years before by stupid whites and it eternally came back to haunt us all. The secretary and I were like Hamlet and Laertes[10] in the final scene, where, because of harm done by one ancestor to another, we were bound to duel to the death. Also because the play must end somewhere.

I went further than forgiving the clerk, I accepted her as a fellow victim of the same puppeteer.

On the streetcar, I put my fare into the box and the conductorette looked at me with the usual hard eyes of white contempt. "Move into the car, please move on in the car." She patted her money changer.

Her Southern nasal accent sliced my meditation and I looked deep into my thoughts. All lies, all comfortable lies. The receptionist was not innocent and neither was I. The whole charade[11] we had played out in that crummy waiting room had directly to do with me, Black, and her, white.

I wouldn't move into the streetcar but stood on the ledge over the conductor, glaring. My mind shouted so energetically that the announcement made my veins stand out, and my mouth tighten into a prune.

---

9. **concocted** [kon kokt' əd]: made up.
10. **Hamlet and Laertes** [ham' lit lā ėr' tēz]: in Shakespeare's *Hamlet*, the prince of Denmark, Hamlet, kills his friend Laertes in a duel at the end of the play.
11. **charade** [shə rād]: meaningless or false action or series of actions.

I WOULD HAVE THE JOB. I WOULD BE A CONDUC-
TORETTE AND SLING A FULL MONEY CHANGER FROM
MY BELT. I WOULD.

The next three weeks were a honeycomb of determination with
apertures[12] for the days to go in and out. The Negro organizations to
whom I appealed for support bounced me back and forth like a
shuttlecock on a badminton court. Why did I insist on that
particular job? Openings were going begging that paid nearly twice
the money. The minor officials with whom I was able to win an
audience thought me mad. Possibly I was.

12. **apertures** [ap′ ər chürz]: openings.

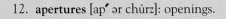

Downtown San Francisco became alien and cold, and the streets I had loved in a personal familiarity were unknown lanes that twisted with malicious[13] intent. Old buildings, whose gray rococo façades housed my memories of the Forty-Niners, and Diamond Lil, Robert Service, Sutter and Jack London, were then imposing structures viciously joined to keep me out. My trips to the streetcar office were of the frequency of a person on salary. The struggle expanded. I was no longer in conflict only with the Market Street Railway but with the marble lobby of the building which housed its offices, and elevators and their operators.

During this period of strain Mother and I began our first steps on the long path toward mutual adult admiration. She never asked for reports and I didn't offer any details. But every morning she made breakfast, gave me carfare and lunch money, as if I were going to work. She comprehended the perversity of life, that in the struggle lies the joy. That I was no glory seeker was obvious to her, and that I had to exhaust every possibility before giving in was also clear.

On my way out of the house one morning she said, "Life is going to give you just what you put in it. Put your whole heart in everything you do, and pray, then you can wait." Another time she reminded me that "God helps those who help themselves." She had a store of aphorisms[14] which she dished out as the occasion demanded. Strangely, as bored as I was with clichés, her inflection gave them something new, and set me thinking for a little while at least. Later when asked how I got my job, I was never able to say exactly. I only knew that one day, which was tiresomely like all the others before it, I sat in the Railway office, ostensibly waiting to be interviewed. The receptionist called me to her desk and shuffled a bundle of papers to me. They were job application forms. She said they had to be filled in triplicate. I had little time to wonder if I had won or not, for the standard questions reminded me of the necessity for dexterous[15] lying. How old was I? List my previous jobs, starting from the last held

13. **malicious** [mə lish′ əs]: cruel and spiteful.
14. **aphorisms** [af′ ə riz′ əmz]: short sentences that express a truth or piece of wisdom.
15. **dexterous** [dek′ stər əs]: skillful.

and go backward to the first. How much money did I earn, and why did I leave the position? Give two references (not relatives).

Sitting at a side table my mind and I wove a cat's ladder of near truths and total lies. I kept my face blank (an old art) and wrote quickly the fable of Marguerite Johnson, aged nineteen, former companion and driver for Mrs. Annie Henderson (a White Lady) in Stamps, Arkansas.

I was given blood tests, aptitude tests, physical coordination tests, and Rorschachs, then on a blissful[16] day I was hired as the first Negro on the San Francisco streetcars.

Mother gave me the money to have my blue serge suit tailored, and I learned to fill out work cards, operate the money changer and punch transfers. The time crowded together and at an End of Days I was swinging on the back of the rackety trolley, smiling sweetly and persuading my charges to "step forward in the car, please."

For one whole semester the streetcars and I shimmied up and scooted down the sheer hills of San Francisco. I lost some of my need for the Black ghetto's shielding-sponge quality, as I clanged and cleared my way down Market Street, with its honky-tonk homes for homeless sailors, past the quiet retreat of Golden Gate Park and along closed undwelled-in-looking dwellings of the Sunset District.

My work shifts were split so haphazardly[17] that it was easy to believe that my superiors had chosen them maliciously. Upon mentioning my suspicions to Mother, she said, "Don't worry about it. You ask for what you want, and you pay for what you get. And I'm going to show you that it ain't no trouble when you pack double."

She stayed awake to drive me out to the car barn at four thirty in the mornings, or to pick me up when I was relieved just before dawn. Her awareness of life's perils convinced her that while I would be safe on the public conveyances, she "wasn't about to trust a taxi driver with her baby."

When the spring classes began, I resumed my commitment with formal education. I was so much wiser and older, so much more

16. **blissful** [blis′ fəl]: extremely happy, joyful.
17. **haphazardly** [hap′ haz′ ərd lē]: without being planned ahead.

independent, with a bank account and clothes that I had bought for myself, that I was sure that I had learned and earned the magic formula which would make me a part of the gay life my contemporaries led.

Not a bit of it. Within weeks, I realized that my schoolmates and I were on paths moving diametrically away from each other. They were concerned and excited over the approaching football games, but I had in my immediate past raced a car down a dark and foreign Mexican mountain. They concentrated great interest on who was worthy of being student body president, and when the metal bands would be removed from their teeth, while I remembered sleeping for a month in a wrecked automobile and conducting a streetcar in the uneven hours of the morning.

Without willing it, I had gone from being ignorant of being ignorant to being aware of being aware. And the worst part of my awareness was that I didn't know what I was aware of. I knew I knew very little, but I was certain that the things I had yet to learn wouldn't be taught to me at George Washington High School.

I began to cut classes, to walk in Golden Gate Park or wander along the shiny counter of the Emporium Department Store. When Mother discovered that I was playing truant, she told me that if I didn't want to go to school one day, if there were no tests being held, and if my school work was up to standard, all I had to do was tell her and I could stay home. She said that she didn't want some white woman calling her up to tell her something about her child that she didn't know. And she didn't want to be put in the position of lying to a white woman because I wasn't woman enough to speak up. That put an end to my truancy, but nothing appeared to lighten the long gloomy day that going to school became.

To be left alone on the tightrope of youthful unknowing is to experience the excruciating beauty of full freedom and the threat of eternal indecision. Few, if any, survive their teens. Most surrender to the vague but murderous pressure of adult conformity. It becomes easier to die and avoid conflicts than to maintain a constant battle with the superior forces of maturity.

Until recently each generation found it more expedient to plead guilty to the charge of being young and ignorant, easier to take the punishment meted out by the older generation (which had itself confessed to the same crime short years before). The command to grow up at once was more bearable than the faceless horror of wavering purpose, which was youth.

The bright hours when the young rebelled against the descending sun had to give way to twenty-four-hour periods called "days" that were named as well as numbered.

The Black female is assaulted in her tender years by all those common forces of nature at the same time that she is caught in the tripartite crossfire of masculine prejudice, white illogical hate and Black lack of power.

The fact that the adult American Negro female emerges a formidable character is often met with amazement, distaste and even belligerence. It is seldom accepted as an inevitable outcome of the struggle won by survivors and deserves respect if not enthusiastic acceptance.

MAYA ANGELOU

Maya Angelou was born in 1928 in St. Louis, Missouri. When she was three years old, her parents divorced and sent Angelou and her brother to live with their grandmother in Stamps, Arkansas. Angelou grew up attending the segregated public school there; her high school years were spent in California. Over the years, she studied music, dance, and drama from private teachers.

Angelou had a hard time as a teenager but never gave up on herself. Today she says, "I believe all things are possible for a human being, and I don't think there's anything in the world I can't do." She has become one of the best-known American writers of books, plays, and poetry. She speaks six languages. She has worked in television and lectured in the United States and Ghana. All her life and work, Angelou believes, is about survival.

74th Street

MYRA COHN LIVINGSTON

East Twelfth Street Ben Shahn, 1946, tempera, 22" x 30"

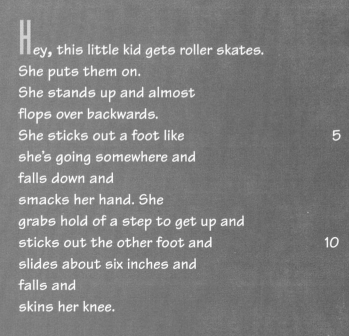

Hey, this little kid gets roller skates.
She puts them on.
She stands up and almost
flops over backwards.
She sticks out a foot like   5
she's going somewhere and
falls down and
smacks her hand. She
grabs hold of a step to get up and
sticks out the other foot and   10
slides about six inches and
falls and
skins her knee.

And then, you know what?

She brushes off the dirt and the   15
blood and puts some
spit on it and then
sticks out the other foot

again.

MYRA COHN LIVINGSTON

Myra Cohn Livingston was born in 1926 in Omaha, Nebraska. Livingston started out as a musician, playing the French horn professionally as a teenager. Then, at eighteen, she published her first poem and began channeling her creativity into writing.

Livingston is also a teacher. She instructs her writing students to "either tell me something I have never heard before or tell me in a new way something I have heard before." Two of her collections are *A Circle of Seasons* and *There Was a Place and Other Poems*.

Above, 1984 Olympic high diving champion Greg Louganis, U.S.A., and right, 1948 Olympic high diving champion Sammy Lee, U.S.A.

THE OLYMPIC GAMES

THEODORE KNIGHT

DETERMINED TO SUCCEED

Not all obstacles are physical. Adversity can take many forms, as the linked stories of Olympic divers Dr. Sammy Lee and Greg Louganis show. Lee was the winner of the gold medal in platform diving and the bronze medal in springboard diving in 1948 and the gold medal in platform diving again in 1952. When Lee captured his second gold medal in 1952 at the age of thirty-two, he went into the record books as the oldest athlete ever to win an Olympic diving medal, but that is not even close to the true measure of his achievement.

Lee was born in California to Korean parents who had fled the Japanese invasion of Korea.[1] Lee's family was too poor to attend the 1932 Games in Los Angeles, but when his father explained what the Olympics were all about, the boy announced that one day he would

1. **Japanese invasion of Korea:** Japan controlled Korea from 1910 until the end of World War II.

be an Olympic champion. "In what sport?" laughed his father. "Gee, I don't know, Pop," the boy replied, "but someday I'll find one." Not long afterward, Lee discovered that he could do things off a diving board that the other kids could not do. Soon he had heavier kids double-bouncing him off the diving board so he could get higher into the air and do more stunts. Diving was fast becoming Lee's passion.

DEALING WITH DISCRIMINATION

In 1936, two things happened that cemented young Lee's determination. The gold medal winner in the marathon[2] was a runner named Kitei Son.[3] Although he was listed as Japanese and running for the Japanese team, Korean-Americans knew that Kitei Son was really Sohn Kee Chung,[4] a Korean forced by the invading Japanese to compete for them. On the victory stand, Chung tore off his Japanese emblem and announced to the world, "I'm Korean, not Japanese." He was immediately seized and whisked away by the Japanese, but not before he had become a hero to Koreans everywhere and especially to young Sammy Lee. The other 1936 Olympian who made an indelible[5] impression on Lee was the black American runner Jesse Owens. Owens had overcome racial prejudice at home and abroad to run brilliantly in the 1936 Olympics. Smarting under the widespread prejudice against Asians in this country, Lee was inspired by Owens's feats and the respect they brought to him.

As a teenager, Lee had difficulty finding pools that would allow him to practice. The public pool in his hometown of Pasadena, California, for example, was open to him only on Mondays. Mondays were designated International Day, when non-whites were allowed to use the facilities. Each Monday evening, it was rumored, the pool was drained and then refilled with clean water. While still a teenager, Lee met and began to train with some of the best divers in the

2. **marathon** [mar′ ə thon]: a race run over a long distance, usually 26 miles, 385 yards.
3. **Kitei Son** [kē′ tā sōn]
4. **Sohn Kee Chung** [sôn kē′ chung]
5. **indelible** [in del′ ə bəl]: permanent.

country, among them several former Olympians. One former champion—Farid Simaika,[6] the Egyptian 1928 silver medalist who had moved to this country—gave Lee a piece of advice that he took to heart. He told the young diver that he might encounter prejudice in competition because he was of Korean descent. Simaika told Lee he would simply have to work twice as hard as other athletes. "You've got to be so much better that they have to give you the medal," Simaika said.

COMPETITION AND A CONTINUING COMMITMENT

Lee began to perfect more complex dives than had ever before been done in competition—forward three-and-a-half somersaults, reverse two-and-a-half somersaults and inward two-and-a-half somersaults. Despite his growing success as a diver and his impressive academic achievements, prejudice pursued Lee even to the Olympic Games themselves. In London in 1948, just as Lee began competition in the platform diving competition, he was told that an

6. **Farid Simaika** [fä rēd′ sim ī′ kä]

American swimming association official had been heard telling the diving judges, "I hope you don't favor that Korean." Only Lee's extra-ordinary confidence and self-control could have enabled him to make one perfect dive after another off that thirty-three-foot diving tower with those vicious words of his fellow countryman ringing in his ears.

Lee won a second gold medal in 1952 in Helsinki, Finland. Although this marked his last Olympic performance, it did not end his close ties to the Olympics. Lee later took time from his medical career to coach a young man named Greg Louganis. Louganis had suffered from a difficult childhood. He was born of Samoan and Swedish parents who gave him up for adoption at birth. He was called nigger by his schoolmates in California because of his dark skin and labeled retarded because he had a severe reading disability called dyslexia.[7] By age thirteen, Louganis was in trouble with the law and addicted to drugs and alcohol. But he also had developed an interest in diving. Lee spotted Louganis diving one day and saw promise in the young man's dives. With Lee's support, Louganis escaped from his difficulties into the world of competitive diving. He showed such promise that he qualified for the Montreal, Canada, Olympics at the age of sixteen. In Montreal in 1976, he finished sixth in the spring-board competition and second in the platform diving. In 1984 at Los Angeles, he carried the day with gold medals in both springboard competition and platform diving, becoming the first diver to win the gold in both events since 1928.

The Seoul[8] Olympics in 1988 represented the third and last ap-pearance in a long and remarkable career for Greg Louganis, and the Games provided a fitting conclusion. By 1988, at twenty-eight years old, Louganis was an old man in diving circles, but he was still the fa-vorite in both diving events. Things began very badly, however, in the preliminaries[9] of the springboard competition. Louganis bounced

---

7. **dyslexia** [dis lek′ sē ə]: a brain problem that causes difficulty in reading.
8. **Seoul** [sōl]: the capital of South Korea.
9. **preliminaries** [pri lim′ ə ner′ ēz]: contests that come before the main event.

hard on the board and launched himself high into the air for a two-and-a-half pike.[10] As he twisted and rolled and then plunged back toward the water, his head slammed into the end of the diving board. Spectators and television viewers alike will never forget the loud, hollow sound of Louganis's head hitting the board, the splash as he tumbled into the water, or the suspenseful moments as everyone waited to see if he would surface. Incredibly, Louganis suffered only an ugly gash in his scalp that was closed with five stitches. He immediately returned to competition and still managed to qualify for the finals. He carried off both gold medals again and became the first man ever to repeat as Olympic champion in both events.

Greg Louganis accepts one of his Olympic gold medals in 1984.

10. **pike** [pīk]: a dive in which the diver bends at the waist, keeps the knees straight, and usually touches the toes.

THEODORE KNIGHT

Theodore Knight was born and grew up in Rhode Island. At one time, Knight managed a large bookstore, but later became a freelance author and editor. Besides *The Olympic Games*, Knight has been writing a book about former President Jimmy Carter. Knight says he admires Carter partly because he didn't just retire but "went on to an important new career" after being president.

Through the Tunnel

DORIS LESSING

Going to the shore on the first morning of the vacation, the young English boy stopped at a turning of the path and looked down at a wild and rocky bay, and then over to the crowded beach he knew so well from other years. His mother walked on in front of him, carrying a bright striped bag in one hand. Her other arm, swinging loose, was very white in the sun. The boy watched that white, naked arm, and turned his eyes, which had a frown behind them, toward the bay and back again to his mother. When she felt he was not with her, she swung around. "Oh, there you are, Jerry!" she said. She looked impatient, then smiled. "Why, darling, would you rather not come with me? Would you rather—" She frowned, conscientiously worrying over what amusements he might secretly be longing for, which she had been too busy or too careless to imagine. He was very familiar with that anxious, apologetic smile. Contrition[1] sent him running after her. And yet, as he ran, he looked back over his shoulder at the wild bay; and all morning, as he played on the safe beach, he was thinking of it.

1. **contrition** [kən trish´ ən]: sorrow for having hurt someone, guilt.

Next morning, when it was time for the routine of swimming and sunbathing, his mother said, "Are you tired of the usual beach, Jerry? Would you like to go somewhere else?"

"Oh, no!" he said quickly, smiling at her out of that unfailing impulse of contrition—a sort of chivalry. Yet, walking down the path with her, he blurted out, "I'd like to go and have a look at those rocks down there."

She gave the idea her attention. It was a wild-looking place, and there was no one there; but she said, "Of course, Jerry. When you've had enough, come to the big beach. Or just go straight back to the villa, if you like." She walked away, that bare arm, now slightly reddened from yesterday's sun, swinging. And he almost ran after her again, feeling it unbearable that she should go by herself, but he did not.

She was thinking, Of course he's old enough to be safe without me. Have I been keeping him too close? He mustn't feel he ought to be with me. I must be careful.

He was an only child, eleven years old. She was a widow. She was determined to be neither possessive nor lacking in devotion. She went worrying off to her beach.

As for Jerry, once he saw that his mother had gained her beach, he began the steep descent to the bay. From where he was, high up among red-brown rocks, it was a scoop of moving bluish green fringed with white. As he went lower, he saw that it spread among small promontories[2] and inlets[3] of rough, sharp rock, and the crisping, lapping surface showed stains of purple and darker blue. Finally, as he ran sliding and scraping down the last few yards, he saw an edge of white surf and the shallow, luminous[4] movement of water over white sand, and, beyond that, a solid, heavy blue.

He ran straight into the water and began swimming. He was a

2. **promontories** [prom′ ən tôr′ ēz]: high points of land extending from the coast into the water.
3. **inlets** [in′ letz]: narrow bays or channels of water extending inland from a large body of water.
4. **luminous** [lü′ mə nəs]: shining, full of light.

good swimmer. He went out fast over the gleaming sand, over a middle region where rocks lay like discolored monsters under the surface, and then he was in the real sea—a warm sea where irregular cold currents from the deep water shocked his limbs.

When he was so far out that he could look back not only on the little bay but past the promontory that was between it and the big beach, he floated on the buoyant surface and looked for his mother. There she was, a speck of yellow under an umbrella that looked like a slice of orange peel. He swam back to shore, relieved at being sure she was there, but all at once very lonely.

On the edge of a small cape that marked the side of the bay away from the promontory was a loose scatter of rocks. Above them, some boys were stripping off their clothes. They came running, naked, down to the rocks. The English boy swam toward them, but kept his distance at a stone's throw. They were of that coast; all of them were burned smooth dark brown and speaking a language he did not understand. To be with them, of them, was a craving that filled his whole body. He swam a little closer; they turned and watched him with narrowed, alert dark eyes. Then one smiled and waved. It was enough. In a minute, he had swum in and was on the rocks beside them, smiling with a desperate, nervous supplication.[5] They shouted cheerful greetings at him; and then, as he preserved his nervous, uncomprehending smile, they understood that he was a foreigner strayed from his own beach, and they proceeded to forget him. But he was happy. He was with them.

They began diving again and again from a high point into a well of blue sea between rough, pointed rocks. After they had dived and come up, they swam around, hauled themselves up, and waited their turn to dive again. They were big boys—men, to Jerry. He dived, and they watched him; and when he swam around to take his place, they made way for him. He felt he was accepted and he dived again, carefully, proud of himself.

Soon the biggest of the boys poised himself, shot down into the

5. **supplication** [sup′ lə kā′ shən]: humble begging.

water, and did not come up. The others stood about, watching. Jerry, after waiting for the sleek brown head to appear, let out a yell of warning; they looked at him idly and turned their eyes back toward the water. After a long time, the boy came up on the other side of a big dark rock, letting the air out of his lungs in a sputtering gasp and a shout of triumph. Immediately the rest of them dived in. One moment, the morning seemed full of chattering boys; the next, the air and the surface of the water were empty. But through the heavy blue, dark shapes could be seen moving and groping.

Jerry dived, shot past the school of underwater swimmers, saw a black wall of rock looming at him, touched it, and bobbed up at once to the surface, where the wall was a low barrier he could see across. There was no one visible; under him, in the water, the dim shapes of the swimmers had disappeared. Then one, and then another of the boys came up on the far side of the barrier of rock, and he understood that they had swum through some gap or hole in it. He plunged down again. He could see nothing through the stinging salt water but the blank rock. When he came up the boys were all on the diving rock, preparing to attempt the feat again. And now, in a panic of failure, he yelled up, in English, "Look at me! Look!" and he began splashing and kicking in the water like a foolish dog.

They looked down gravely, frowning. He knew the frown. At moments of failure, when he clowned to claim his mother's attention, it was with just this grave, embarrassed inspection that she rewarded him. Through his hot shame, feeling the pleading grin on his face like a scar that he could never remove, he looked up at the group of big brown boys on the rock and shouted, *"Bonjour! Merci! Au revoir! Monsieur, monsieur!"*[6] while he hooked his fingers round his ears and waggled them.

Water surged into his mouth; he choked, sank, came up. The rock, lately weighted with boys, seemed to rear up out of the water as their weight was removed. They were flying down past him, now, into the water; the air was full of falling bodies. Then the rock was empty in the hot sunlight. He counted one, two, three. . . .

At fifty, he was terrified. They must all be drowning beneath him, in the watery caves of the rock! At a hundred, he stared around him at the empty hillside, wondering if he should yell for help. He counted faster, faster, to hurry them up, to bring them to the surface quickly, to drown them quickly—anything rather than the terror of counting on and on into the blue emptiness of the morning. And then, at a hundred and sixty, the water beyond the rock was full of boys blowing like brown whales. They swam back to the shore without a look at him.

He climbed back to the diving rock and sat down, feeling the hot roughness of it under his thighs. The boys were gathering up their bits of clothing and running off along the shore to another promontory. They were leaving to get away from him. He cried openly, fists in his eyes. There was no one to see him, and he cried himself out.

It seemed to him that a long time had passed, and he swam out to where he could see his mother. Yes, she was still there, a yellow spot under an orange umbrella. He swam back to the big rock, climbed up, and dived into the blue pool among the fanged and angry

6. *"Bonjour! Merci! Au revoir! Monsieur, monsieur!"* [bōn zhür′ mār sē′ ō rə vwär′ mə syœ′]: French for "Hello! Thank you! Good bye! Mister, mister!"

boulders. Down he went, until he touched the wall of rock again. But the salt was so painful in his eyes that he could not see.

He came to the surface, swam to shore and went back to the villa to wait for his mother. Soon she walked slowly up the path, swinging her striped bag, the flushed, naked arm dangling beside her. "I want some swimming goggles," he panted, defiant[7] and beseeching.

She gave him a patient, inquisitive look as she said casually, "Well, of course, darling."

But now, now, now! He must have them this minute, and no other time. He nagged and pestered until she went with him to a shop. As soon as she had bought the goggles, he grabbed them from her hand as if she were going to claim them for herself, and was off, running down the steep path to the bay.

Jerry swam out to the big barrier rock, adjusted the goggles, and dived. The impact of the water broke the rubber-enclosed vacuum, and the goggles came loose. He understood that he must swim down to the base of the rock from the surface of the water. He fixed the goggles tight and firm, filled his lungs, and floated, face down, on the water. Now, he could see. It was as if he had eyes of a different kind—fish eyes that showed everything clear and delicate and wavering in the bright water.

Under him, six or seven feet down, was a floor of perfectly clean, shining white sand, rippled firm and hard by the tides. Two grayish shapes steered there, like long, rounded pieces of wood or slate. They were fish. He saw them nose toward each other, poise motionless, make a dart forward, swerve off, and come around again. It was like a water dance. A few inches above them the water sparkled as if sequins were dropping through it. Fish again—myriads[8] of minute fish, the length of his fingernail, were drifting through the water, and in a moment he could feel the innumerable tiny touches of them against his limbs. It was like swimming in flaked silver. The great rock the big boys had swum through rose sheer out of the white

---

7. **defiant** [di fī′ ənt]: challenging authority, bold.
8. **myriads** [mir′ ē ədz]: a very great number.

sand—black, tufted lightly with greenish weed. He could see no gap in it. He swam down to its base.

Again and again he rose, took a big chestful of air, and went down. Again and again he groped over the surface of the rock, feeling it, almost hugging it in the desperate need to find the entrance. And then, once, while he was clinging to the black wall, his knees came up and he shot his feet out forward and they met no obstacle. He had found the hole.

He gained the surface, clambered about the stones that littered the barrier rock until he found a big one, and, with this in his arms, let himself down over the side of the rock. He dropped, with the weight, straight to the sandy floor. Clinging tight to the anchor of stone, he lay on his side and looked in under the dark shelf at the place where his feet had gone. He could see the hole. It was an irregular, dark gap; but he could not see deep into it. He let go of his anchor, clung with his hands to the edges of the hole, and tried to push himself in.

He got his head in, found his shoulders jammed, moved them in sidewise, and was inside as far as his waist. He could see nothing ahead. Something soft and clammy touched his mouth; he saw a dark frond[9] moving against the grayish rock, and panic filled him. He thought

9. **frond:** a large leaf.

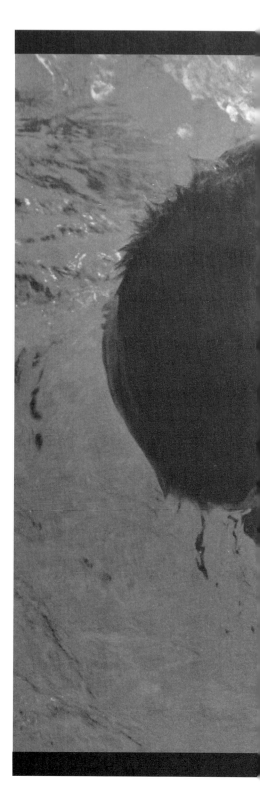

of octopuses, of clinging weed. He pushed himself out backward and caught a glimpse, as he retreated, of a harmless tentacle of seaweed drifting in the mouth of the tunnel. But it was enough. He reached the sunlight, swam to shore, and lay on the diving rock. He looked down into the blue well of water. He knew he must find his way through that cave, or hole, or tunnel, and out the other side.

First, he thought, he must learn to control his breathing. He let himself down into the water with another big stone in his arms, so that he could lie effortlessly on the bottom of the sea. He counted. One, two, three. He counted steadily. He could hear the movement of blood in his chest. Fifty-one, fifty-two. . . . His chest was hurting. He let go of the rock and went up into the air. He saw that the sun was low. He rushed to the villa and found his mother at her supper. She said only "Did you enjoy yourself?" and he said "Yes."

All night the boy dreamed of the water-filled cave in the rock, and as soon as breakfast was over he went to the bay.

That night, his nose bled badly. For hours he had been underwater, learning to hold his breath, and now he felt weak and dizzy. His mother said, "I shouldn't overdo things, darling, if I were you."

That day and the next, Jerry exercised his lungs as if everything, the whole of his life, all that he would become, depended upon it. Again his nose bled at night, and his mother insisted on his coming with her the next day. It was a torment to him to waste a day of his careful self-training, but he stayed with her on that other beach, which now seemed a place for small children, a place where his mother might lie safe in the sun. It was not his beach.

He did not ask for permission, on the following day, to go to his beach. He went, before his mother could consider the complicated rights and wrongs of the matter. A day's rest, he discovered, had improved his count by ten. The big boys had made the passage while he counted a hundred and sixty. He had been counting fast, in his fright. Probably now, if he tried, he could get through that long tunnel, but he was not going to try yet. A curious, most unchildlike persistence, a controlled impatience, made him wait. In the meantime, he lay underwater on the white sand, littered now by stones he had brought down from the upper air, and studied the entrance to the tunnel. He knew every jut and corner of it, as far as it was possible to see. It was as if he already felt its sharpness about his shoulders.

He sat by the clock in the villa, when his mother was not near, and checked his time. He was incredulous and then proud to find he could hold his breath without strain for two minutes. The words "two minutes," authorized by the clock, brought close the adventure that was so necessary to him.

In another four days, his mother said casually one morning, they must go home. On the day before they left, he would do it. He would do it if it killed him, he said defiantly to himself. But two days before they were to leave—a day of triumph when he increased his count by fifteen—his nose bled so badly that he turned dizzy and had to lie limply over the big rock like a bit of seaweed, watching the thick red blood flow on to the rock and trickle slowly down to the sea. He was frightened. Supposing he turned dizzy in the tunnel? Supposing he died there, trapped? Supposing—his head went around, in the hot sun, and he almost gave up. He thought he would return to the house and lie down, and next summer, perhaps, when he had another year's growth in him—*then* he would go through the hole.

But even after he had made the decision, or thought he had, he found himself sitting up on the rock and looking down into the water; and he knew that now, this moment, when his nose had only just stopped bleeding, when his head was still sore and throbbing—this was the moment when he would try. If he did not do it now, he never would. He was trembling with fear that he would not go; and he was trembling with horror at that long, long tunnel under the rock, under the sea. Even in the open sunlight, the barrier rock seemed very wide and very heavy; tons of rock pressed down on where he would go. If he died there, he would lie until one day—perhaps not before next year—those big boys would swim into it and find it blocked.

He put on his goggles, fitted them tight, tested the vacuum. His hands were shaking. Then he chose the biggest stone he could carry and slipped over the edge of the rock until half of him was in the cool, enclosing water and half in the hot sun. He looked up once at the empty sky, filled his lungs once, twice, and then sank fast to the bottom with the stone. He let it go and began to count. He took the edges of the hole in his hands and drew himself into it, wriggling his shoulders in sidewise as he remembered he must, kicking himself along with his feet.

Soon he was clear inside. He was in a small rock-bound hole filled with yellowish-gray water. The water was pushing him up against the roof. The roof was sharp and pained his back. He pulled himself along with his hands—fast, fast—and used his legs as levers. His head knocked against something; a sharp pain dizzied him. Fifty, fifty-one, fifty-two. . . . He was without light, and the water seemed to press upon him with the weight of rock. Seventy-one, seventy-two. . . . There was no strain on his lungs. He felt like an inflated balloon, his lungs were so light and easy, but his head was pulsing.

He was being continually pressed against the sharp roof, which felt slimy as well as sharp. Again he thought of octopuses, and wondered if the tunnel might be filled with weed that could tangle him. He gave himself a panicky, convulsive[10] kick forward, ducked his head, and swam. His feet and hands moved freely, as if in open water. The hole must have widened out. He thought he must be swimming fast, and he was frightened of banging his head if the tunnel narrowed.

A hundred, a hundred and one. . . . The water paled. Victory filled him. His lungs were beginning to hurt. A few more strokes and he would be out. He was counting wildly; he said a hundred and fifteen, and then, a long time later, a hundred and fifteen again. The water was a clear jewel-green all around him. Then he saw, above his head, a crack running up through the rock. Sunlight was falling through it, showing the clean, dark rock of the tunnel, a single mussel shell, and darkness ahead.

He was at the end of what he could do. He looked up at the crack as if it were filled with air and not water, as if he could put his mouth to it to draw in air. A hundred and fifteen, he heard himself say inside his head—but he had said that long ago. He must go on

---

10. **convulsive** [kən vul′ siv]: unintentionally violent and fast.

into the blackness ahead, or he would drown. His head was swelling, his lungs cracking. A hundred and fifteen, a hundred and fifteen pounded through his head, and he feebly clutched at rocks in the dark, pulling himself forward, leaving the brief space of sunlit water behind. He felt he was dying. He was no longer quite conscious. He struggled on in the darkness between lapses into unconsciousness. An immense, swelling pain filled his head, and then the darkness cracked with an explosion of green light. His hands, groping forward, met nothing; and his feet, kicking back, propelled him out into the open sea.

He drifted to the surface, his face turned up to the air. He was gasping like a fish. He felt he would sink now and drown; he could not swim the few feet back to the rock. Then he was clutching it and pulling himself up on to it. He lay face down, gasping. He could see nothing but a red-veined, clotted dark. His eyes must have burst, he thought; they were full of blood. He tore off his goggles and a gout of blood went into the sea. His nose was bleeding, and the blood had filled the goggles.

He scooped up handfuls of water from the cool, salty sea, to splash on his face, and did not know whether it was blood or salt water he tasted. After a time, his heart quieted, his eyes cleared, and he sat up. He could see the local boys diving and playing half a mile away. He did not want them. He wanted nothing but to get back home and lie down.

In a short while, Jerry swam to shore and climbed slowly up the path to the villa. He flung himself on his bed and slept, waking at the sound of feet on the path outside. His mother was coming back. He rushed to the bathroom, thinking she must not see his face with bloodstains, or tearstains, on it. He came out of the bathroom and met her as she walked into the villa, smiling, her eyes lighting up.

"Have a nice morning?" she asked, laying her hand on his warm brown shoulder a moment.

"Oh, yes, thank you," he said.

"You look a bit pale." And then, sharp and anxious, "How did you bang your head?"

"Oh, just banged it," he told her.

She looked at him closely. He was strained; his eyes were glazed-looking. She was worried. And then she said to herself, Oh, don't fuss! Nothing can happen. He can swim like a fish.

They sat down to lunch together.

"Mummy," he said, "I can stay under water for two minutes—three minutes, at least." It came bursting out of him.

"Can you, darling?" she said. "Well, I shouldn't overdo it. I don't think you ought to swim any more today."

She was ready for a battle of wills, but he gave in at once. It was no longer of the least importance to go to the bay.

DORIS LESSING

Doris Lessing was born in 1919 to a British family living in Iran. She grew up in the African country then called Southern Rhodesia, now Zimbabwe. She never visited England until she was thirty. Lessing became a writer in Africa, and she writes of life there.

Lessing left school early and began writing at eighteen. (She tore up her first six novels.) Her first published novel was a success. She went on to write more, including science fiction and nonfiction. Lessing has always been concerned with politics and social issues. But short stories are her favorite form.

As a recognized writer, Lessing tried an experiment. She wrote two novels under the pseudonym Jane Somers. They were published, but the critics ignored them and the publisher's lack of advertising kept them from selling well. It showed, Lessing said, why it can be so hard for unknown writers to become known, even when they write well!

Cornfield with Cypresses Vincent Van Gogh, 1889, oil on canvas, 28 ¹/₂″ x 36″, National Gallery, London

For Poets
AL YOUNG

Stay beautiful
but dont stay down underground too long
Dont turn into a mole
or a worm
or a root   5
or a stone

Come on out into the sunlight
Breathe in trees
Knock out mountains
Commune[1] with snakes   10
& be the very hero of birds

Dont forget to poke your head up
& blink
Think
Walk all around   15
Swim upstream

Dont forget to fly

---

1. **commune** [kə myün′]: communicate
   effortlessly as with a good friend.

AL YOUNG

Al Young was born in 1939 in Ocean Springs, Mississippi. His father
was an auto worker and professional musician. Following in his footsteps,
Young started out at eighteen as a jazz musician, playing guitar and flute
and singing professionally while attending the University of Michigan. He
also began writing poetry.

Young's first book, *Dancing: Poems,* was published in 1969; he
published his first novel the following year. Critics have praised him for
capturing the rhythms of African American music in his writing. They have
also praised his creation of convincing characters who struggle with the
problems of real life that face everyone.

You can find "For Poets" and other poems in Young's book, *The Song
Turning Back into Itself.*

RAYMOND'S RUN

TONI CADE BAMBARA

I don't have much work to do around the house like some girls. My mother does that. And I don't have to earn my pocket money by hustling; George runs errands for the big boys and sells Christmas cards. And anything else that's got to get done, my father does. All I have to do in life is mind my brother Raymond, which is enough.

Sometimes I slip and say my little brother Raymond. But as any fool can see he's much bigger and he's older too. But a lot of people call him my little brother cause he needs looking after cause he's not quite right. And a lot of smart mouths got lots to say about that too, especially when George was minding him. But now, if anybody has anything to say to Raymond, anything to say about his big head, they have to come by me. And I don't play the dozens or believe in standing around with somebody in my face doing a lot of talking. I much rather just knock you down and take my chances even if I am a little girl with skinny arms and a squeaky voice, which is how I got the name Squeaky. And if things get too rough, I run. And as anybody can tell you, I'm the fastest thing on two feet.

There is no track meet that I don't win the first place medal. I used to win the twenty-yard dash when I was a little kid in kindergarten. Nowadays, it's the fifty-yard dash. And tomorrow I'm subject to run the quarter-meter relay all by myself and come in first, second, and third. The big kids call me Mercury[1] cause I'm the swiftest thing in the neighborhood. Everybody knows that—except two people who know better, my father and me. He can beat me to Amsterdam Avenue with me having a two fire-hydrant headstart and him running with his hands in his pockets and whistling. But that's private information. Cause can you imagine some thirty-five-year-old man stuffing himself into PAL[2] shorts to race little kids? So as far as everyone's concerned, I'm the fastest and that goes for Gretchen, too, who has put out the tale that she is going to win the first-place medal this year. Ridiculous. In the second place, she's got short legs. In the third place, she's got freckles. In the first place, no one can beat me and that's all there is to it.

1. **Mercury** [mėr′ kyər ē]: in Roman myths, the fast-moving messenger of the gods.
2. **PAL:** Police Athletic League.

I'm standing on the corner admiring the weather and about to take a stroll down Broadway so I can practice my breathing exercises, and I've got Raymond walking on the inside close to the buildings, cause he's subject to fits of fantasy and starts thinking he's a circus performer and that the curb is a tightrope strung high in the air. And sometimes after a rain he likes to step down off his tightrope right into the gutter and slosh around getting his shoes and cuffs wet. Then I get hit when I get home. Or sometimes if you don't watch him he'll dash across traffic to the island in the middle of Broadway and give the pigeons a fit. Then I have to go behind him apologizing to all the old people sitting around trying to get some sun and getting all upset with the pigeons fluttering around them, scattering their newspapers and upsetting the waxpaper lunches in their laps. So I keep Raymond on the inside of me, and he plays like he's driving a stage coach which is O.K. by me so long as he doesn't run me over or interrupt my breathing exercises, which I have to do on account of I'm serious about my running, and I don't care who knows it.

Now some people like to act like things come easy to them, won't let on that they practice. Not me. I'll high-prance down 34th Street like a rodeo pony to keep my knees strong even if it does get my mother uptight so that she walks ahead like she's not with me, don't know me, is all by herself on a shopping trip, and I am somebody else's crazy child. Now you take Cynthia Procter for instance. She's just the opposite. If there's a test tomorrow, she'll say something like, "Oh, I guess I'll play handball this afternoon and watch television tonight," just to let you know she ain't thinking about the test. Or like last week when she won the spelling bee for the millionth time, "A good thing you got 'receive,' Squeaky, cause I would have got it wrong. I completely forgot about the spelling bee." And she'll clutch the lace on her blouse like it was a narrow escape. Oh, brother. But of course when I pass her house on my early morning trots around the block, she is practicing the scales on the piano over and over and over and over. Then in music class she always lets herself get bumped around so she falls accidently on purpose onto the piano stool and is so surprised to find herself sitting there that she decides just for fun to try out the ole keys. And what do you know—Chopin's[3] waltzes just spring out of her fingertips and she's the most surprised thing in the world. A regular prodigy.[4] I could kill people like that. I stay up all night studying the words for the spelling bee. And you can see me any time of day practicing running. I never walk if I can trot, and shame on Raymond if he can't keep up. But of course he does, cause if he hangs back someone's liable to walk up to him and get smart, or take his allowance from him, or ask him where he got that great big pumpkin head. People are so stupid sometimes.

So I'm strolling down Broadway breathing out and breathing in on counts of seven, which is my lucky number, and here comes Gretchen and her sidekicks: Mary Louise, who used to be a friend of mine when she first moved to Harlem from Baltimore and got beat up by everybody till I took up for her on account of her mother and my mother used to sing in the same choir when they were young girls, but people ain't grateful, so now she hangs out with the new girl Gretchen and talks about me like a dog; and Rosie, who is as fat as I am skinny and has a big mouth where Raymond is concerned and is too stupid to know that there is not a big deal of difference between herself and Raymond and that she can't afford to throw stones. So they are steady coming up Broadway and I see right away that it's going to be one of those Dodge City scenes cause the street ain't that big and they're close to the buildings just as we are. First I think I'll step into the candy store and look over the new comics and let them pass. But that's chicken and I've got a reputation to consider. So then I think I'll just walk straight on through them or even over them if necessary. But as they get to me, they slow down. I'm ready to fight, cause like I said I don't feature a whole lot of chit-chat, I much prefer to just knock you down right from the jump and save everybody a lotta precious time.

"You signing up for the May Day[5] races?" smiles Mary Louise,

3. **Chopin** [shō′pan]: Polish composer and pianist of the nineteenth century who lived in France.
4. **prodigy** [prod′ ə jē]: young person who is extremely brilliant and talented.
5. **May Day:** May 1, in some countries the traditional day for celebrating spring with games and dancing around a pole decorated with colored ribbons.

only it's not a smile at all. A dumb question like that doesn't deserve an answer. Besides, there's just me and Gretchen standing there really, so no use wasting my breath talking to shadows.

"I don't think you're going to win this time," says Rosie, trying to signify with her hands on her hips all salty, completely forgetting that I have whupped her behind many times for less salt than that.

"I always win cause I'm the best," I say straight at Gretchen who is, as far as I'm concerned, the only one talking in this ventriloquist-dummy routine. Gretchen smiles, but it's not a smile, and I'm thinking that girls never really smile at each other because they don't know how and don't want to know how and there's probably no one to teach us how, cause grown-up girls don't know either. Then they all look at Raymond who has just brought his mule team to a standstill. And they're about to see what trouble they can get into through him.

"What grade you in now, Raymond?"

"You got anything to say to my brother, you say it to me, Mary Louise Williams of Raggedy Town, Baltimore."

"What are you, his mother?" sasses Rosie.

"That's right, Fatso. And the next word out of anybody and I'll be *their* mother too." So they just stand there and Gretchen shifts from one leg to the other and so do they. Then Gretchen puts her hands on her hips and is about to say something with her freckle-face self but doesn't. Then she walks around me looking me up and down but keeps walking up Broadway, and her sidekicks follow her. So me and Raymond smile at each other and he says, "Gidyap" to his team and I continue with my breathing exercises, strolling down Broadway toward the ice man on 145th with not a care in the world cause I am Miss Quicksilver herself.

I take my time getting to the park on May Day because the track meet is the last thing on the program. The biggest thing on the program is the May Pole dancing, which I can do without, thank you, even if my mother thinks it's a shame I don't take part and act like a girl for a change. You'd think my mother'd be grateful not to have to make me a white organdy[6] dress with a big satin sash and buy me new white

6. **organdy** [ôr′ gən dē′]: fine, transparent material.

baby-doll shoes that can't be taken out of the box till the big day. You'd think she'd be glad her daughter ain't out there prancing around a May Pole getting the new clothes all dirty and sweaty and trying to act like a fairy or a flower or whatever you're supposed to be when you should be trying to be yourself, whatever that is, which is, as far as I am concerned, a poor Black girl who really can't afford to buy shoes and a new dress you only wear once a lifetime cause it won't fit next year.

I was once a strawberry in a Hansel and Gretel pageant when I was in nursery school and didn't have no better sense than to dance on tiptoe with my arms in a circle over my head doing umbrella steps and being a perfect fool just so my mother and father could come dressed up and clap. You'd think they'd know better than to encourage that kind of nonsense. I am not a strawberry. I do not dance on my toes. I run. That is what I am all about. So I always come late to the May Day program, just in time to get my number pinned on and lay in the grass till they announce the fifty-yard dash.

I put Raymond in the little swings, which is a tight squeeze this year and will be impossible next year. Then I look around for Mr. Pearson, who pins the numbers on. I'm really looking for Gretchen if you want to know the truth, but she's not around. The park is jam-packed. Parents in hats and corsages and breast-pocket handkerchiefs peeking up. Kids in white dresses and light-blue suits. The parkees unfolding chairs and chasing the rowdy kids from Lenox as if they had no right to be there. The big guys with their caps on backwards, leaning against the fence swirling the basketballs on the tips of their fingers, waiting for all these crazy people to clear out the park so they can play. Most of the kids in my class are carrying bass drums and glockenspiels[7] and flutes. You'd think they'd put in a few bongos or something for real like that.

Then here comes Mr. Pearson with his clipboard and his cards and pencils and whistles and safety pins and fifty million other things he's always dropping all over the place with his clumsy self. He sticks

---

7. **glockenspiels** [glok′ ən spēlz]: musical instruments played by striking two hammers on metal bells, bars, or tubes that are mounted in two rows in a frame.

out in a crowd because he's on stilts. We used to call him Jack and the Beanstalk to get him mad. But I'm the only one that can outrun him and get away, and I'm too grown for that silliness now.

"Well, Squeaky," he says, checking my name off the list and handing me number seven and two pins. And I'm thinking he's got no right to call me Squeaky, if I can't call him Beanstalk.

"Hazel Elizabeth Deborah Parker," I correct him and tell him to write it down on his board.

"Well, Hazel Elizabeth Deborah Parker, going to give someone else a break this year?" I squint at him real hard to see if he is seriously thinking I should lose the race on purpose just to give someone else a break. "Only six girls running this time," he continues, shaking his head sadly like it's my fault all of New York didn't turn out in sneakers. "That new girl should give you a run for your money." He looks around the park for Gretchen like a periscope in a submarine movie. "Wouldn't it be a nice gesture if you were . . . to ahhh . . . "

I give him such a look he couldn't finish putting that idea into words. Grownups got a lot of nerve sometimes. I pin number seven to myself and stomp away, I'm so burnt. And I go straight for the track and stretch out on the grass while the band winds up with "Oh, the Monkey Wrapped His Tail Around the Flag Pole," which my teacher calls by some other name. The man on the loudspeaker is calling everyone over to the track and I'm on my back looking at the sky, trying to pretend I'm in the country, but I can't, because even grass in the city feels hard as sidewalk, and there's just no pretending you are anywhere but in a "concrete jungle" as my grandfather says.

The twenty-yard dash takes all of two minutes cause most of the little kids don't know no better than to run off the track or run the wrong way or run smack into the fence and fall down and cry. One little kid, though, has got the good sense to run straight for the white ribbon up ahead so he wins. Then the second-graders line up for the thirty-yard dash and I don't even bother to turn my head to watch cause Raphael Perez always wins. He wins before he even begins by psyching the runners, telling them they're going to trip on their shoelaces and fall on their faces or lose their shorts or something,

which he doesn't really have to do since he is very fast, almost as fast as I am. After that is the forty-yard dash which I use to run when I was in first grade. Raymond is hollering from the swings cause he knows I'm about to do my thing cause the man on the loudspeaker has just announced the fifty-yard dash, although he might just as well be giving a recipe for angel food cake cause you can hardly make out what he's sayin for the static. I get up and slip off my sweat pants and then I see Gretchen standing at the starting line, kicking her legs out like a pro. Then as I get into place I see that ole Raymond is on line on the other side of the fence, bending down with his fingers on the ground just like he knew what he was doing. I was going to yell at him but then I didn't. It burns up your energy to holler.

Every time, just before I take off in a race, I always feel like I'm in a dream, the kind of dream you have when you're sick with fever and feel all hot and weightless. I dream I'm flying over a sandy beach in the early morning sun, kissing the leaves of the trees as I fly by. And there's always the smell of apples, just like in the country when I was little and used to think I was a choo-choo train, running through the fields of corn and chugging up the hill to the orchard. And all the time I'm dreaming this, I get lighter and lighter until I'm flying over the beach again, getting blown through the sky like a feather that weighs nothing at all. But once I spread my fingers in the dirt and crouch over the Get on Your Mark, the dream goes and I am solid again and am telling myself, Squeaky you must win, you must win, you are the fastest thing in the world, you can even beat your father up Amsterdam if you really try. And then I feel my weight coming back just behind my knees then down to my feet then into the earth and the pistol shot explodes in my blood and I am off and weightless again, flying past the other runners, my arms pumping up and down and the whole world is quiet except for the crunch as I zoom over the gravel in the track. I glance to my left and there is no one. To the right, a blurred Gretchen, who's got her chin jutting out as if it would win the race all by itself. And on the other side of the fence is Raymond with his arms down to his side and the palms tucked up behind him, running in his very own style, and it's the first time I ever saw that and I almost stop to watch my brother Raymond on his first run. But the white ribbon is bouncing toward me and I tear past it, racing into the distance till my feet with a mind of their own start digging up footfuls of dirt and brake me short. Then all the kids standing on the side pile on me, banging me on the back and slapping my head with their May Day programs, for I have won again and everybody on 151st Street can walk tall for another year.

"In first place . . . " the man on the loudspeaker is clear as a bell now. But then he pauses and the loudspeaker starts to whine. Then static. And I lean down to catch my breath and here comes Gretchen walking back, for she's overshot the finish line too, huffing and puffing with her hands on her hips taking it slow, breathing in steady time like a real pro and I sort of like her a little for the first time. "In first place . . . " and then three or four voices get all mixed up on the loudspeaker and I dig my sneaker into the grass and stare at Gretchen who's staring back, we both wondering just who did win. I can hear old Beanstalk arguing with the man on the loudspeaker and then a few others running their mouths about what the stopwatches say. Then I hear Raymond yanking at the fence to call me and I wave to shush him, but he keeps rattling the fence like a gorilla in a cage like in them gorilla movies, but then like a dancer or something he starts climbing up nice and easy but very fast. And it occurs to me, watching how smoothly he climbs hand over hand and remembering how he looked running with his arms down to his side and with the wind pulling his mouth back and his teeth showing and all, it occurred to me that Raymond would make a very fine runner. Doesn't he always keep up with me on my trots? And he surely knows how to breathe in counts of seven cause he's always doing it at the dinner table, which drives my brother George up the wall. And I'm smiling to beat the band cause if I've lost this race, or if me and Gretchen tied, or even if I've won, I can always retire as a runner and begin a whole new career as a coach with Raymond as my champion. After all, with a little more study I can beat Cynthia and her phony self at the spelling bee. And if I bugged my mother, I could get piano lessons and become a star. And I have a big rep as the baddest thing around.

And I've got a roomful of ribbons and medals and awards. But what has Raymond got to call his own?

So I stand there with my new plans, laughing out loud by this time as Raymond jumps down from the fence and runs over with his teeth showing and his arms down to the side, which no one before him has quite mastered as a running style. And by the time he comes over I'm jumping up and down so glad to see him—my brother Raymond, a great runner in the family tradition. But of course everyone thinks I'm jumping up and down because the men on the loudspeaker have finally gotten themselves together and compared notes and are announcing "In first place—Miss Hazel Elizabeth Deborah Parker." (Dig that.) "In second place—Miss Gretchen P. Lewis." And I look over at Gretchen wondering what the "P" stands for. And I smile. Cause she's good, no doubt about it. Maybe she'd like to help me coach Raymond; she obviously is serious about running, as any fool can see. And she nods to congratulate me and then she smiles. And I smile. We stand there with this big smile of respect between us. It's about as real a smile as girls can do for each other, considering we don't practice real smiling every day, you know, cause maybe we too busy being flowers or fairies or strawberries instead of something honest and worthy of respect . . . you know . . . like being people.

TONI CADE BAMBARA

Toni Cade Bambara was born in 1939 in New York City and grew up there, graduating from Queens College. Bambara became a civil rights activist, a professor of English and African American studies, an editor of anthologies of African American literature, and an author. At the same time, she has never stopped working in community programs.

"Raymond's Run" is one of the stories you'll find in Bambara's first book, *Gorilla, My Love*.

ALBERTO RÍOS

February, and the wind has begun
Milk cartons moving along the curb,
An occasional wrapper, Baby Ruth.

The young tree bends in a hoeing.
Cirrus[1] clouds, sparrows, jet trailings: 5
Each puts a line on the sky. February

Kites, too, their shapes: the way three
Boys have taken their baseball fields
Into the air, flying them on strings.

When I flew my kite I shouted, louder,   10
Anything, strong, boy wild and rocks:
February was here. I was helping.

1. **cirrus** [sir′ əs]: high, thin, feathery, white clouds.

ALBERTO RÍOS

Alberto Ríos was born in 1952 in Nogales, Arizona. Since his father was born in Mexico and his mother in England, he is a first-generation American. Ríos majored in English literature and creative writing at the University of Arizona. He wrote poetry and later began also writing fiction and drama.

Ríos speaks Spanish and has written a great deal from the Mexican side of his heritage. England, he has said, "is supposed to always wait for me." But the death of his English grandmother, a woman he had never met, was a reminder that parts of life do not wait forever.

Ríos's poem "What a Boy Can Do" is from his book *Teodoro Luna's Two Kisses*.

THUMBPRINT

In the heel of my thumb
are whorls,[1] whirls, wheels
in a unique design:
mine alone.
What a treasure to own!   5
My own flesh, my own feelings.
No other, however grand or base,
can ever contain the same.
My signature,   10
thumbing the pages of my time.
My universe key,
my singularity.
Impress, implant,
I am myself,   15
of all my atom parts I am the sum.
And out of my blood and my brain
I make my own interior weather,
my own sun and rain.
Imprint my mark upon the world,   20
whatever I shall become.

---

1. **whorls** [hwôrlz]: circular fingerprint patterns on
   the fingertips by which people can be identified.

EVE MERRIAM

Eve Merriam [1916-1992] was born in Philadelphia, Pennsylvania. She began her long and busy career in New York as a radio writer for Columbia Broadcasting System during the early l940s. She published her first book of poems, *Family Circle*, in l946, and wrote for *Glamour* and other fashion magazines. Throughout her life Merriam wrote steadily, publishing many books of poetry as well as fiction and nonfiction.

Merriam's many interests included travel, sports, and living in the city. Most of all, she loved her work. "I am fortunate that my work is my main pleasure," she once said, "and, while I find all forms of writing absorbing, I like poetry as the most immediate and richest form of communication."

Merriam loved humor, too. One of her last books is called *Chortles: New and Selected Wordplay Poems*.

PICTURES ON A ROCK

One spring day a few years before the Rough Rock Demonstration School was opened, a five-year-old Navajo[1] boy named Fred Bia was watching the family sheep flock in the arid[2] countryside near the little town. It was his daily chore to follow the sheep as they drifted over the red, rocky earth in their endless search for grass and the leaves of semi-desert plants. He had covered this ground so many times that he no longer paid any attention to where he was, his thoughts wandering as he moved slowly with the animals.

When he saw the rock in front of him, he knew he was in a place that he had not been before, and he could not believe his eyes. The big red rock was covered with drawings of people and animals. Fred stood very still as he stared at them, and an excitement he had never felt before raced through his blood. Who had made these pictures? When? He had no idea. There were no drawings on the other rocks around him, only those he was staring at. He was almost hypnotized and though he had no way of knowing it, in that moment Fred Bia, Navajo artist, was born.

When he finally looked away from the rock, he saw that his sheep were nearly out of sight, and he ran to catch up with them. But he did not forget the drawings on the rock. He thought about them that night, and the next day he returned to the rock. The same feeling of excitement came back to him. He picked up a small chalky stone, went to a large rock nearby, and did his best to copy the drawings of people and animals he saw on the red rock.

1. **Navajo** [nav′ ə hō]: Native American nation of New Mexico, Arizona, and Utah.
2. **arid** [ar′ id]: dry, having little rainfall.

Later that day in another part of the rocky semidesert where he had followed his sheep, Fred drew the pictures from memory on other rocks. In the days and weeks that followed he drew other pictures, some from his imagination, some from the things in nature around him. By the time he entered first grade, Fred's pictures covered many of the big rocks around Rough Rock.

In school Fred discovered crayons, and fortunately he had teachers who quickly saw that the boy had a real drawing ability and an unusual fascination with making pictures. They encouraged him and saw that he had plenty of crayons and paper. When Fred went to high school in Chinle and Fort Wingate[3] the encouragement continued, and his powers as a pictorial artist grew.

After he graduated from high school, he was accepted as a student at the Institute of American Indian Art in Santa Fe.[4] Fred began in elementary classes, but his instructors at this special school for promising Indian artists moved him to advanced classes.

Fred spent two years at the art institute and then embarked on a career as a professional artist. Today he is one of a small number of Indian artists whose work sells steadily and brings substantial prices. Major fame remains in the future, but he has established himself as a solid professional painter whose work is in a number of western art galleries and museums and in such private collections as that of famous country-music singer Johnny Cash.

"I want to be thought of as a painter, not as a Navajo painter or an Indian painter," Fred says. "But I draw my subjects from the Navajo world, the people and the land, because that is what I know."

Fred returned to Rough Rock to live, and for the past three years he has given much of his time to illustrating a series of Navajo social studies books that the Rough Rock Demonstration School is producing for grades kindergarten through twelve. The books will be made available to all Navajo schools. His powerful black-and-white

3. **Chinle and Fort Wingate** [chin′ lē]: a town on the Navajo Reservation in northeastern Arizona; a town on the Navajo Reservation in northwestern New Mexico.
4. **Sante Fe** [san′ tə fā′]: capital of New Mexico, situated in the northern part of the state.

drawings of Black Mesa,[5] Shiprock,[6] and other Navajo landmarks, as well as faithful visual portraits of Navajo people and cultural objects, will give Navajo schoolchildren a new and exciting look at themselves and their world as Navajos.

Fred sometimes talks about the day that changed his life, the day he saw the drawings on the rock in the desert. He never learned how the drawings got there or what they were. He does not think they were ancient pictographs, although there are many of them in Navajo country. They may have been the work of a shaman[7] or medicine man, but Fred does not think they were that either.

"They were just there, and I saw them," he says. "I am very glad I did."

Navajo artist Fred Bía and his daughter

5. **Black Mesa** [mā′ sə]: a mesa, a high plateau with a flat top and steep sides, in New Mexico.
6. **Shiprock:** a town on the Navajo Reservation in northwestern New Mexico.
7. **shaman** [shä′ mən]

BRENT ASHABRANNER

Brent Ashabranner was born in 1921 in Shawnee, Oklahoma. He began writing as a young boy and published his first short story when he was twenty. Although Ashabranner has written more short stories, most of his writing has been nonfiction—some coauthored with his friend Russell Davis.

Ashabranner writes of the people he has come to know and their lives in the places where they live. He has drawn on his many years of travel and work in a score of countries around the world.

One of Ashabranner's books is a memoir, *The Times of My Life,* that tells of his experiences, from his Oklahoma childhood during the Great Depression through his volunteer work with the Peace Corps during the 1960s.

On SHARK'S TOOTH BEACH

E. L. KONIGSBURG

My dad is Hixon of Hixon's Landing, the fishing camp down on the intracoastal waterway just across Highway A1A. Our camp isn't a fancy one. Just two coolers, one for beer and one for bait, plus four boats and eight motors that we rent out.

Dad was raised on a farm in Nebraska, but he joined the Navy and signed on for the war in Vietnam[1] and came back knowing two things. One, he hated war, and two, he loved the sea. Actually, he came back with two loves. The other one was my mother. There wasn't *any* way *any*one could get him to settle *any*where that was far from the ocean when he got out of the service, so he bought this small stretch of land in north Florida, and we've been there for all of my life that I can remember.

Dad's got this small pension[2] for getting wounded over in Nam, so between what we sell, what we rent and what the government sends, we do all right. We're not what you're likely to call rich, but we are all right. Mom doubts that we'll ever make enough money to pay for a trip to her native country of Thailand, but she doesn't seem to mind. She says that it is more important to love where you're at than to love where you're from.

1. **Vietnam** [vē et′ näm′]: country in Southeast Asia where the United States was involved in a war from about 1957 to 1973.
2. **pension** [pen′ shən]: here, a fixed amount of money paid regularly by the government to a war veteran, especially one who has been wounded.

Mom makes and sells sandwiches for the fishermen. She does a right good job on them, I can tell you. There is this about Mom's sandwiches: you don't have to eat halfway through to the middle to find out what's between the bread, and once you get hold of a bite, you don't have to guess at whether it is egg salad or tuna that you're eating. The filling is high in size and in flavor.

The town next door to us is spreading south toward our landing, and both Mom and Dad say that our property will be worth a pretty penny in a few years. But both of them always ask, "What's a pretty penny worth when you can't buy anything prettier than what you already have?" I have to agree. Maybe because I don't know anything else, but I can't imagine what it would be like not to have a sandbox miles and miles long and a pool as big as an ocean for a playground across the street—even if the street is a highway. I can't ever remember going to sleep but that I heard some water shushing and slurping or humming and hollering for a lullaby.

Last spring, just as the days were getting long enough that a person could both start and finish something between the time he got home from school and the time he went to bed, I went out onto our dock and I saw this guy all duded up from a catalogue. Now that the town has grown toward us, we have more of these guys than we used to. When you've been in the business of fishing all your life, you come to know the difference between fishermen and guys who have a hobby. Here are some of the clues:

1. The hat. A real fisherman's hat is darkened along the edges where the sweat from his hand leaves marks. A non-fisherman's hat has perfect little dent marks in it.

2. The smile. Real fishermen don't smile while they're fishing unless someone tells them a joke. Real fishermen wear their faces in the same look people wear when they are in church—deliberate and far-off—the way they do when they don't want to catch the eye of the preacher. The only time that look changes is when they take a swig of beer and then it changes only a little and with a slow rhythm like watching instant replay on television. Non-fishermen twitch their necks around like pigeons, which are very

citified birds, and non-fishermen smile a lot.

3.   The umbrella. Real fishermen don't have them.

This old guy sat on a wooden-legged, canvas-bottom folding campstool that didn't have any salt burns on it anywhere and put his rod into one of the holders that Dad had set up along the dock railing. Then he held out his hand and called out, "Hey, boy, do you know what I've got here?"

I walked on over to him and said, "Name's Ned."

"What's that?" he asked, cupping his hand over his ear so that the breeze wouldn't blow it past him.

"I said that my name is Ned," I repeated.

"All right, Ed," he said. "I have a question for you. Do you know what this is, boy?"

"Name's Ned," I repeated. I looked down at the palm of his hand and saw a medium-sized shark's tooth from a sand shark. "Not bad," I said.

"But do you know what it is, boy?" he asked.

I could tell that it wasn't the kind of question where a person is looking for an answer; it was the kind of question where a person just wants you to look interested long enough so that he can get on with telling you the answer. I decided that I wouldn't play it that way even if he was a customer. Three *boys* in a row made me mean, so I said, "Medium-sized sand."

"What's that?" he shouted, cupping his hand over his ear again.

"Medium-sized sand," I repeated louder.

"That's a shark's tooth," he said, clamping his hand shut.

Shoot! I knew that it was a shark's tooth. I was telling him what *kind* it was and what size it was.

"That is a fossilized[3] shark's tooth, boy," he said. "Found it just across the street."

"Name's Ned," I told him, and I walked away.

Sharks' teeth wash up all the time at the beach just across the road from Hixon's Landing. There's a giant fossil bed out in the

---

3. **fossilized** [fos′ ə līzd]: changed by time into a rock-like material.

ocean somewheres, and a vent from it leads right onto our beach. When the undertow[4] gets to digging up out of that fossil bed and the tide is coming in, all kinds of interesting things wash in. Besides the sharks' teeth, there are also pieces of bones that wash up. I collect the backbones, the vertebraes, they're called; they have a hole in them where the spinal column went through. I have a whole string of them fixed according to size.

I collect sharks' teeth, too. I have been doing it for years. Mom started me doing it. It was Mom who made a study of them and found what kind of animal they might come from. Mom has these thorough ways about her. Dad says that Mom is smarter'n a briar and prettier'n a movie star.

Mom fixes the sharks' teeth that we collect into patterns and fastens them down onto a velvet mat and gets them framed into a shadowbox frame. She sells them down at the gift shop in town. And the gift shop isn't any tacky old gift shop full of smelly candles and ashtrays with the name of our town stamped on it. It's more like an art gallery. Matter of fact, it is called *The Artists' Gallery,* and Mom is something of an artist at how she makes those sharks' teeth designs. Some of the really pretty sharks' teeth Mom sells to a jeweler who sets them in gold for pendants. When she gets two pretty ones that match, he makes them into earrings.

4. **undertow** [un′ dər tō′]: the backward flow of water from waves breaking on the shore.

When I find her a really special or unusual one, Mom says to me, "Looks like we got a trophy, Ned." When we get us a trophy, one that needs investigating or one that is just downright super special, we don't sell it. Shoot! We don't even think about selling it. There's nothing that bit of money could buy that we'd want more than having that there trophy.

Most everyone who comes to Hixon's Landing knows about Mom and me being something of authorities on fossils, especially sharks' teeth, so I figured that this old dude would either go away and not come back or hang around long enough to find out. Either way, I figured that I didn't need to advertise for myself and my mom.

The next day after school there was the old fellow again. I wouldn't want to sound braggy or anything, but I could tell that he was standing there at the end of our dock waiting for me to come home from school.

"Hi," I said.

"Well, boy," he said, "did you have a good day at school?"

"Fair," I answered. I decided to let the *boy* ride. I figured that he couldn't hear or couldn't remember or both. "Catch anything?" I asked.

"No, not today," he said. "Matter of fact I was just about to close up shop." Then he began reeling in, looking back over his shoulder to see if I was still hanging around. He didn't even bother taking the hook off his line; he just dumped rod and reel down on the dock and stuck out his hand to me and said, "Well, son, you can call me President Bob."

"What are you president of?" I asked.

"President of a college, upstate Michigan. But I'm retired now."

"Then you're not a president," I said.

"Not at the moment, but the title stays. The way that people still call a retired governor, *Governor*. You can call me President Bob instead of President Kennicott. Bob is more informal, but I wouldn't want you to call me just Bob. It doesn't seem respectful for a boy to call a senior citizen just Bob."

"And you can call me Ned," I said. "That's my name."

"All right, son," he said.

"After the first day, I don't answer to *son* or to *boy*," I said.

"What did you say your name was, son?"

Shoot! He had to learn. So I didn't answer.

"What is your name again?"

"Ned."

"Well, Ned, would you like to take a walk on the beach and hunt for some of those sharks' teeth?"

"Sure," I said.

He must have counted on my saying yes, because the next thing I see is him dropping his pants and showing me a pair of skinny white legs with milky blue veins sticking out from under a pair of bathing trunks.

As we walked the length of the dock, he told me that he was used to the company of young men since he had been president of a college. "Of course, the students were somewhat older," he said. Then he laughed a little, like punctuation. I didn't say anything. "And, of course, I didn't often see the students on a one-to-one basis." I didn't say anything. "I was president," he added. He glanced over at me, and I still didn't say anything. "I was president," he added.

"There's supposed to be some good fishing in Michigan," I said.

"Oh, yes! Yes, there is. Good fishing. Fine fishing. Sportsmen's fishing."

We crossed A1A and got down onto the beach from a path people had worn between the dunes, and I showed him how to look for sharks' teeth in the coquina.[5] "There's nothing too much to learn," I said. "It's mostly training your eye."

He did what most beginners do, that is, he picked up a lot of wedge-shaped pieces of broken shell, mostly black, thinking they were fossil teeth. The tide was just starting on its way out, and that is the best time for finding sharks' teeth. He found about eight of them, and two of them were right nice sized. I found fourteen myself and three of mine were bigger than anything he collected. We compared, and I could tell that he was wishing he had mine, so I gave him one

---

5. **coquina** [kō kē′ nə]: soft, porous limestone formed of fragments of sea shells and corals.

of my big ones. It wasn't a trophy or anything like that because I would never do that to Mom, that is, give away a trophy or a jewelry one.

President Bob was waiting for me the next day and the day after that one. By the time Friday afternoon came, President Bob gave up on trying to pretend that he was fishing. He'd just be there on the dock, waiting for me to take him sharks' tooth hunting.

"There's no magic to it," I told him. "You can go without me."

"That's all right, Ned," he said, "I don't mind waiting."

On Saturday I had a notion to sleep late and was in the process of doing just that when Mom shook me out of my sleep and told me that I had a visitor. It was President Bob, and there he was standing on his vanilla legs right by my bedroom door. He had gotten tired of waiting for me on the dock. It being Saturday, he had come early so's we could have more time together.

Mom invited him in to have breakfast with me, and while we ate, she brought out our trophy boxes. Our trophies were all sitting on cotton in special boxes like the ones you see butterflies fixed in inside a science museum. Mom explained about our very special fossils.

"Oh, yes," President Bob said. Then, "Oh, yes," again. Then after he'd seen all our trophies and had drunk a second cup of coffee, he said, "We had quite a fine reference library in my college. I am referring to the college of which I was president. Not my alma mater, the college I attended as a young man. We had quite a fine library, and I must confess I used it often, so I am not entirely unfamiliar with these things."

That's when I said, "Oh, yes," except that it came out, "Oh, yeah!" and that's when Mom swiped my foot under the table.

President Bob plunked his empty cup down on the table and said, "Well, come on now, Ned, time and tide wait for no man. Ha! Ha!"

I think that I've heard someone say that at least four times a week. Everyone says it. Dad told me that it was a proverb,[6] an old, old saying. And I can tell you that it got old even before I reached my second birthday.

6. **proverb** [prov′ ĕrb]: a short, wise saying used for a long time by many people.

When we got down to the beach, President Bob brought out a plastic bag and flung it open like a bag boy at the supermarket. But there wasn't much to fill it with that day because the currents had shifted and weren't churning up the fossil bed.

"I suppose you'll be going to church tomorrow," he said.

"Yes," I answered.

"I think I'll do some fishing in the morning. I'll probably have had enough of that by noon. I'll meet you at the dock about twelve-thirty. We can get started on our shark's tooth hunt then."

"Sorry," I said. "I help Mom with the sandwiches and then we clean things up and then we go to late services. Sunday is our busiest day."

"Of course it is," he said.

Mom and I got back about one-thirty and changed out of our good clothes before Dad came in as he always does on Sundays to grab some lunch before the men start coming back and he has to get busy with washing down motors and buying. (What he buys is fish from the men who have had a specially good run. Dad cleans them and sells them to markets back in town or to people who drive on out toward the beach of a Sunday. Sometimes, he gets so busy buying and cleaning that Mom and I pitch right in and give him a hand.)

Dad had not quite finished his sandwiches and had just lifted his beer when he got called out to the dock. There was this big haul of bass that some men were wanting to sell.

Mom and I were anxious to finish our lunch and clean up so's we could go on out and see if Dad would be needing some help when President Bob presented himself at the screen door to our kitchen.

"Knock, knock," he said, pressing his old face up against the screen. The minute we both looked up he opened the door without even an *if you please* and marched into our kitchen on his frosted icicle legs. "I think you're going to be interested in what I found today," he said. "Very interested."

Mom smiled her customer smile and said, "We are having very busy day, please to excuse if I continue with work."

"That's perfectly all right," President Bob said. "You're excused." Then he sat down at the table that Mom was wiping off. He held up the placemat and said, "Over here, Mama-san. You missed a spot."

Mom smiled her customer smile again and wiped the spot that he had pointed to, and President Bob put the placemat back down and emptied the contents of his plastic bag right on top of it. He leaned over the pile and using his forefinger began to comb through it. "Ah! here," he said. He picked up a small black thing between his thumb and forefinger and said to Mom, "Come here, Mama-san." *Mama-san* is some kind of Japanese for *mama*. A lot of people call my mom that, but she says it's okay because it is a term of respect, and a lot of people think that all Orientals are Japanese. Sometimes these same people call me Boy-san, which is to *boy* what Mama-san is to *mama*. They call me that because I have dark slanted eyes just like Mom's, except that hers are prettier.

"Look at this," President Bob said. "Look at it closely. I suspect that it is the upper palate[7] of an extinct species of deep water fish."

Mom took it from his hand and looked at it and said, "Dolphin tooth." She put it back down and walked to the sink where she

7. **palate** [pal′ it]: roof of the mouth.

continued right on with washing up the dishes. She automatically handed me a towel to dry.

President Bob studied the dolphin's tooth and said to Mom, "Are you sure?"

She smiled and nodded.

"Quite sure?"

She nodded.

He asked once more, and she nodded again. Then he began poking through his collection again and came up with another piece. He beckoned to Mom to look at it closer, and she dried her hands and did that.

"Shell," she said.

"Oh, I beg to differ with you," he said.

"Shell," Mom said, looking down at it, not bothering to pick it up.

"Are you sure?"

She nodded.

"Quite sure?"

She nodded again, and I came over and picked it up off the table and held it up and broke it in two. I thought that President Bob was going to arrest me. "A piece of fossil that thick wouldn't break that easy. It's a sure test," I said.

"There are fragile fossils, I'm sure," President Bob said.

"I suppose so," I said. "But that shell ain't fossilized. Piece of fossil that thick wouldn't ever break that easy." I could see that you had to repeat yourself with President Bob. "That shell ain't fossilized."

"*Ain't* is considered very bad manners up North," President Bob said.

Shoot! *Bad manners* are considered bad manners down South, I thought. But I didn't say anything. President Bob kept sorting through his bag of stuff, studying on it so hard that his eyes winched up and made his bottom jaw drop open.

Mom finished washing the dishes, and I finished drying, and we asked if we could be excused, and President Bob told us (in our own kitchen, mind) that it was perfectly all right, but would we please

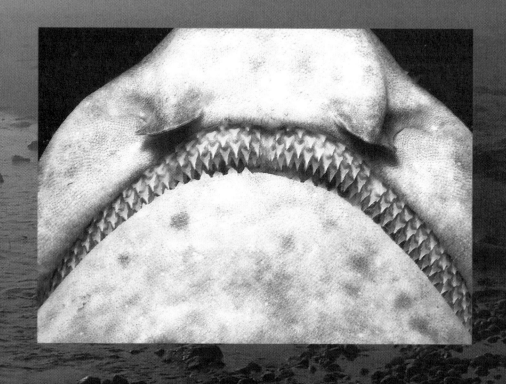

fetch him a glass of ice water before we left. We fetched it. He said, "Thank you. You may go now." I suppose that up North it's good manners to give people orders in their own house if you do it with *please* and *thank you* and no *ain'ts*.

It rained on Monday and it rained again on Tuesday, so I didn't see President Bob again until Wednesday after school. He was waiting for me at the end of the dock with his plastic sandwich bag already partly full. "Well," he said, "I guess I got a bit of a head start on you today."

I looked close at his bag and saw that he had a couple of nice ones—not trophies—but nice.

"I have homework," I said. "I can't walk the beaches with you today."

"What subject?"

"Math."

"Maybe I can help you. Did I tell you that I was president of a college."

"Really?" I said in my fakiest voice. "I think I better do my homework by myself."

"I'll wait for you," he said. "I promise I won't hunt for anything until you come back out."

"It'll probably take me the rest of daylight to do it," I said.

"Math must be hard for you," he said. "Always was my strongest subject."

"It's not hard for me," I lied. "I just have a lot of it."

"Let me show you what I found today," he said.

"I don't think I have the time."

"Just take a minute."

Before I could give him another polite no, he had spread the contents of his bag over the railing of the dock. I looked things over real good. I knew he was watching me, so I wouldn't let my eyes pause too long on any one thing in particular. "Very nice," I said. "I've got to go now."

As I turned to walk back to our house, he called, "See you tomorrow."

The next day I didn't even walk to the dock. Instead I walked around to the side door of our house and threw my books on the wicker sofa on the screened porch and went up to my room and changed into my cut-offs. I had a plan; I was going to go back out the side door and walk a bit to the north before crossing the highway and climbing over the dunes onto the beach. I knew a place where a sandbar often formed, and Mom and I sometimes went there. When I was little, she'd put me in the sloop[8] behind the sandbar, like at a wading pool at a regular Holiday Inn. As I got older, we'd go there on lazy days and take a picnic lunch and sift through the coquina of the sandbar. We've found about four trophies there. Not about, exactly four. Of the four, the first one was the most fun because it was the one we found by accident.

I felt if I could get out of the house and head north, I could escape President Bob and dig up some trophies that would make him flip.

But I didn't escape. When I came downstairs after changing my clothes, there he was sitting on the wicker sofa, his blueberry ripple

8. **sloop** [slüp]: a sailboat, usually having one sail.

legs crossed in front of him. He was leafing through my math book.

I told him hello.

He smiled at me. "Yes, yes, yes," he said, "I know exactly how it is to have to sit in school all day and have to hold your water. I am quite used to the habits of young men. I was president of a liberal arts college in Michigan." He noticed that I was wearing my cut-offs, my usual beachcombing outfit, so he slapped his thighs and set them to shimmying like two pots of vanilla yogurt. "I see you're ready. Let's get going. The tide's halfway out already, and as they say, 'Time and tide wait for no man.' Tide was better a few hours ago. I found a couple of real beauties. Locked them in the glove compartment of my car."

I walked with him to the beach, and we began our hunt. He wasn't bending over for falsies very much any more. Each time he bent over, he yelled, "Got one!" and then he'd hold it up in the air and wouldn't put it in his bag until I nodded or said something or both. President Bob ended up with about twenty teeth, one vertebra bone, and of the twenty, one was a real trophy, an inch long, heavy root and the whole edge serrated[9] with nothing worn away. A real trophy.

I found eight. Three of them were medium, four of them were itty-bitty and one had the tip crushed off.

I got up early the next day and checked the tide; it was just starting out. Good, I thought. I crossed the road and ran out onto the beach, rolling up my pajama bottoms as I walked along. The tide was just right; it was leaving long saw-tooth edges of coquina, and I managed to collect eight decent-sized teeth and one right-good-sized one before I ran back home and hosed off my feet and got dressed for school. I stuffed my collection into pockets of my cut-offs. I had to skip breakfast, a fact that didn't particularly annoy me until about eleven o'clock. That afternoon, for every two times President Bob stooped down and yelled, "Got one!" I did it three times.

On Friday I didn't want to skip breakfast again, and my mother for sure didn't want me to, so President Bob was way ahead.

9. **serrated** [ser′ ā tid]: notched like the edge of a saw.

On Saturday I got up before dawn and dressed and sat on our dock until I saw the first thin line of dawn. Dawn coming over the intracoastal is like watching someone draw up a Venetian blind. On a clear day the sky lifts slowly and evenly, and it makes a guy feel more than okay to see it happen. But on that Saturday, I sat on the dock just long enough to make sure that daylight was to the east of me before I crossed the highway and began heading north. Shoot! I think that if the Lord had done some skywriting that morning, I wouldn't have taken the time to read it, even if it was in English.

Finally, I climbed to the top of a tall dune and walked up one and down another. I was heading for a place between the dunes about a mile to the north. I knew that during spring, when the moon was new, there was a tidewater[10] between two of the dunes. Sharks' teeth got trapped in it, and sometimes Mom and I would go there if there was a special size she was looking for to finish an arrangement. You had to dig down into the coquina, and it wasn't much fun finding sharks' teeth this way instead of sauntering along the beach and happening to find them. But sometimes it was necessary.

I dug.

I dug and I dug and I dug.

I put all my findings into a clam shell that I found, and I dug, and I dug, and I dug. I felt the sun hot on my back, and I still dug. I had my back to the ocean and my face to the ground and for all I knew there was no sky and no sea and no sand and no colors. There was nothing, nothing and nothing except black, and that black was the black of fossil teeth.

I had filled the clam shell before I stopped digging. I sorted the teeth and put the best ones—there were fourteen of them—in my right side pocket—the one with a button—and I put all the smaller ones in my back pocket and started back toward home, walking along the strand. I figured that I had a good head start on the day and on President Bob. I would pepper my regular findings with the ones I had just dug up. I'd mix the little ones in with the fourteen big ones.

10. **tidewater** [tīd′ wô′ tər]: low-lying land along a seacoast through which the tide flows.

But, I decided, smiling to myself, I'd have a run of about eight big ones in a row just to see what he would do.

My back felt that it was near to burning up, and I looked toward the ocean, and it looked powerful good. The morning ocean in the spring can be as blue as the phony color they paint it on a geography book map. Sometimes there are dark patches in it, and the gulls sweep down on top of the dark spots. I decided that I needed to take a dip in that ocean. I half expected a cloud of steam to rise up off my back. I forgot about time and tide and sharks' teeth and ducked under the waves and licked the salt off my lips as I came back up.

I was feeling pretty good, ready to face President Bob and the world, and then I checked my pockets and found that about half the supply from my back pocket had tumbled out, and I had lost two big ones. I was pretty upset about that, so I slowed down on my walk back home. I crouched down and picked up shell pieces, something I thought that I had outgrown, but that is about how anxious I was not to let anything get by me. I found a couple of medium-sized ones and put them in my back pocket and began a more normal walk when my trained eye saw a small tooth right at the tide line.

I reached down to pick it up, figuring that, if nothing else, it would add bulk to my collection the way they add cereal to hot dog meat. I didn't have any idea how many baby teeth I had lost out of my back pocket.

When I reached down to pick up that little tooth, it didn't come up immediately, and I began to think that maybe it was the tip of a really big one. I stooped down and carefully scraped away the wet sand and saw that there were several teeth together. The tide was rushing back up to where I was, so I laid my hand flat down on the ground and shoveled up a whole fistful of wet, cool sand.

I walked back to the dune and gently scraped away the sand with the forefinger of my other hand, and then I saw what I had.

There were several teeth, and they were attached to a piece of bone, a piece of jaw bone. There was a space between the third tooth and the fourth, and the smallest tooth, the one on the end that I had first seen, was attached to the jaw bone by only a thin edge.

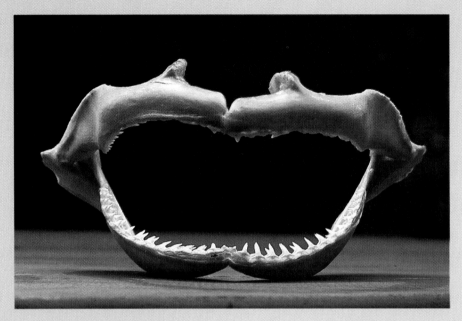

I had never seen such a trophy. I felt that the spirit of the Lord had come mightily upon me, like Samson.[11] Except that I had the jawbone of a shark and not the jawbone of an ass. And I wanted to smite[12] only one president, not a thousand Philistines.

I didn't run the rest of the way home. I was too careful for that. I walked, holding that trophy in my hand, making certain that it didn't dry out before I could see if the weak tooth was fossilized onto the bone.

I called to Mom when I came into the house and when she appeared at the door to the screened porch, I uncurled my fingers one by one until the whole bone and all four of the teeth were showing. I watched Mom's face, and it was like watching the dawn I had missed.

"Ah, Ned," she said, "it is the Nobel Prize[13] of trophies." We walked into the kitchen. She wet a good wad of paper towels and

---

11. **Samson** [sam′ sən]: a very strong man whose story is in the Bible; he used the jawbone of an ass to kill one thousand men in the army of the enemy Philistines.
12. **smite** [smīt]: strike with a weapon to cause serious injury or death.
13. **Nobel Prize** [nō bel′]: a yearly prize given to people who have done outstanding work in science, the arts, or for the good of humanity.

lifted the jawbone carefully from my hand and put it down on that pad of paper. And then we sat down at the kitchen table and I told her about how I found it, and I told it all to her in detail. Dad came in and Mom asked me to tell him, and I did and she listened just as hard the second time.

We ate our breakfast, and afterwards, we wet the paper towels again and moved the trophy onto a plastic placemat on the kitchen table. Mom looked at it through the magnifying glass and then handed me the glass so that I could look at it, too.

While we were studying it hard like that, President Bob came to the screen door and said, "Knock, knock."

Mom nodded at me, her way of letting me know that I was supposed to invite him on in.

"Well, well," he said. "Are we ready for today's treasure hunt?"

"I guess so," I said, as easy as you please, moving a little to the left so that he could catch a glimpse of what Mom and I were looking at.

He gave it a glance and then another one right quick.

Mom and I looked at each other as he came closer and closer to the table. He studied that trophy from his full height and from behind a chair. Next thing, he moved in front of the chair. And next after that he sat down in the chair. And then, not taking his eyes off that trophy, he held his hand out for the magnifying glass and Mom took it from me and gave it to him.

The whole time he did this, I watched his face. His eyes squinched up and his jaw dropped open and his nostrils flared. It was like watching a mini-movie called *Jealousy and Greed.*

I could feel myself smiling. "Found it this morning," I said.

Then I didn't say anything anymore. And I stopped smiling.

I thought about his face, and that made me think about mine. If his face was a movie called *Jealousy and Greed*, I didn't like the words I could put to mine.

I gently pushed the placemat closer to President Bob. "Look at it," I said. "Look at it good." I waited until his eyes were level with mine. "It's for you," I said. "It's a present from me."

"Why, thank you, boy," he said.

"Name's Ned," I answered, as I walked around to the other side of the table and emptied my pockets. "Do you think we can make something pretty out of these?" I asked Mom.

She gave me a Nobel Prize of a smile for an answer. President Bob didn't even notice, he was so busy examining the jawbone with which he had been smitten.

E. L. KONIGSBURG

Elaine Lobl Konigsburg was born in 1930 in New York City and grew up in a small mill town in Pennsylvania. She became a chemist before she became a writer—because, she says, "I was good at it." There was no guidance counselor at her high school, and she was the first person in her family to go to college; she knew no one who made a living from writing. At that time, you went to college to become a professional—such as a teacher or an engineer—who could make a living. But eventually, through teaching, Konigsburg found her way to writing.

Most of Konigsburg's amusing and serious books are for young people. "On Shark's Tooth Beach" is one of the five short stories in her book *Throwing Shadows*. Each story, set in a different place, will draw you into the experience of a different young character.

Asking Big Questions About the Literature

How can I discover my unique qualities?

LITERATURE STUDY

Point of View

Point of view is the way a story is told. When a story is told using pronouns such as *I, me, we,* or *us,* the author is using the *first-person* point of view. When the events of a story are told using pronouns such as *he, she, him, her,* or *them,* the author is using the *third-person* point of view.

Choose a literature selection from this unit and identify its point of view. Then rewrite part of it using a different point of view. (*See "Point of View" on page 118.*)

Write a
THANK-YOU NOTE

Write a thank-you note to a character or an author of one of the literature selections in this unit who has inspired you with a unique quality. Explain how the character or author revealed this quality to you and what you plan to do as a result.

COMPARE & CONTRAST

With a partner, discuss the qualities of several characters in the literature in this unit. Then make a chart like the one shown to compare and contrast the qualities of different characters. Use the chart to help you write a short essay comparing and contrasting the characters.

Selection Title	Character	Qualities
"Raymond's Run"	Squeaky	determined self-disciplined confident committed

How can I improve my unique qualities?

Write an
ADVERTISEMENT

With a group, make a list of real people in the news and characters in this unit who have improved themselves by strengthening qualities they already had. Then imagine one of them is running for political office. Write an advertisement for the candidate's campaign, pointing out how he or she has personally improved. Try out your ad on another group. How would its members vote?

Conflict

A **conflict** is a problem or struggle faced by a character. The conflict can be *internal*—within the character. Or it can be *external*—between the character and another person, nature, or society.

Make a comic strip or story board showing how one character from a literature selection in this unit dealt with a problem and ended up a better person because of it. (*See "Conflict" on page 119.*)

Improvement Scale

With a partner, discuss characters you've read about in the literature selections in this unit who have tried to improve themselves. How did they try? How well did they succeed? Make a Quality Improvement Scale like the one shown. Rate different characters with the same quality. Or rate different qualities of one character. The example is for Ned in "On Shark's Tooth Beach."

Ned's Quality Improvement Scale

	none	a little	some	a lot
friendly			X	
generous				X
tolerant				X
observant			X	

Asking Big Questions About the Literature

How can I share my unique qualities?

ADVICE COLUMN

Share something you've learned with a person who might benefit from your experience. With a partner, choose a character from this unit who could use your advice. What problems does the character face? What similar problems have you solved? Write an advice column. One partner can write the character's letter, explaining the problem and asking for advice. The other can write the columnist's reply.

Reach Out

In "Pictures on a Rock," an artist shares his talent with the world. Other characters in this unit make a contribution to the world. With some classmates, discuss which characters these are and what they do.

What quality or ability do you have that might help one of the characters in the literature selections you've read? Write a letter to that character, offering what you'd like to share.

LITERATURE STUDY

Conflict

In literature, how characters deal with the main problem or **conflict** reveals their inner qualities.

With a group, discuss how characters from this unit use their inner qualities to deal with conflict. List their qualities in character wheels like the one here. Then take turns playing the different characters, answering your classmates' questions about how you solve problems. Let your classmates identify which character you are. (*See "Conflict" on page 119.*)

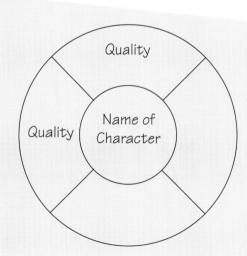

How does the world affect my unique qualities?

An Equation

Choose a character from one of the selections in this unit and set up an equation like the one shown for Penelope in "Young Ladies Don't Slay Dragons." In the first half circle, list things that affect the character. In the second half circle, list the character's inner qualities. Then, in the full circle, write the sum of both halves: the results in the character's life, such as goals achieved or lessons learned.

Influences:
- Other people's assumptions challenge Penelope to prove herself

Outside World

+

Character's Inner Qualities

Penelope is:
- determined
- alert
- brave

=

Results for Character

- success in meeting challenge
- sense of achievement
- increased confidence
- happiness

Tell Your Own Story

With a group, discuss how the world affects the unique qualities of characters in this unit. Then write a short essay about a time in your own life when your unique qualities were affected by your world.

LITERATURE STUDY

Point of View

In fiction, a narrator who identifies himself or herself as *I* is using the *first-person* **point of view**. A narrator who uses pronouns like *he, she,* and *they* is using the third-person point of view.

Write one first-person and one third-person description of the same event from a story in this unit. (*See "Point of View" on page 118.*)

NOW Choose a Project!

Three projects about becoming yourself are described on the following pages.

1 Writing Workshop

Heroes: who are they? We all know them when we find them in the movies or in the stories we read and tell. They're the ones everyone looks up to. But *who* are the people we call heroes? Are they somehow different from the rest of us? How did they get to be heroes? And *where* are they? Do they all live in Texas, or the White House, or Hollywood? Is it possible that ordinary people—such as you and people you know—can also be heroes by using their unique qualities to help others?

This project will give you a chance to decide what heroism is. Your **purpose** will be to write an eyewitness description of a real event that you observed when an ordinary person become a hero. Your **audience** will be the readers of the school newspaper or a local magazine.

Prewriting
THINKING ABOUT HEROISM

What is heroism? Can someone be naturally heroic? What's the difference between a hero and a daredevil? In your journal, write questions such as these about real-life heroism. Write one-sentence answers.

Next make a list of actual heroic acts you've seen or participated in. If you can't think of any, think again: maybe you didn't consider the act heroic at the time. Maybe you did something ordinary that "saved the day" for someone. This list may help you think of an event.

Heroism
- Saving an animal
- Defending a friend
- Helping someone in need

VISUALIZING

Your challenge is to describe every detail of the heroic act. Choose details that will help a reader imagine what happened. Imagine you're a film-maker whose pictures are made of words. Your details should bring to life all the sights, sounds, smells, and other parts of the event. Close your eyes and picture the whole event as vividly as possible. Then jot down a list of as many details as you remember.

Deciding

WHY, WHO, AND HOW

You can't decide *how* to describe the details of the heroic event until you know your **purpose**—*why* you're writing—and your **audience**—*who* your readers will be. Are you writing to describe some event? Are you writing for friends your own age, or for strangers of all ages and backgrounds, or for a group with special interests? Knowing your audience and purpose will help you decide whether to be formal or informal, humorous or serious.

Drafting

....

YOUR EYEWITNESS DESCRIPTION

Your eyewitness description should have three main parts: an introduction, a body, and a conclusion.

- In the **introduction,** try describing the setting: where and when the event takes place. Michelle Parisi, a student writer, introduces her description on page 110 by presenting a very ordinary setting—a school. She also tells the reader the names of the main characters and the person who will perform the heroic act—Maria.

- In the **body** of your eyewitness description, describe the parts of the event in the order in which they happened. Use some transitions, such as *first, next, later,* and *afterward,* to help readers keep track. Then go back to your list of details and be sure you've included them. To bring your description to life, try including some figurative language like similes and metaphors. Michelle, for example, compares Maria's classmates to a pack of wolves: "Instead of teenagers, they now looked more like a wolf pack in search of prey to rip to shreds." Finally remember to include dialogue—what people said during the incident—if it's appropriate.

- In the **conclusion,** tell your readers the results of the heroic action and leave them with some food for thought. It might be a lesson learned from the experience or an update on the heroic person's life since the event. Keep it short.

- Finally give your eyewitness description a **title.** You might want to make a list of ten or more possibilities before choosing a title that fits the purpose and tone of your report. It should spark the reader's interest without giving away too much information.

Revising
YOUR EYEWITNESS DESCRIPTION

Invite a partner or a group to read and respond to your eyewitness description. You may want to ask questions like these:

- Does the opening draw you into the event? Is it too long?
- Do the descriptive details help you picture what happened?
- Are there any clichés—overused expressions—that spoil the freshness of my description?
- Is the conclusion clear?

Based on your friends' suggestions, make some changes to improve your work. Read the student model on pages 110-111 for an example of a successful eyewitness description.

Editing
YOUR EYEWITNESS DESCRIPTION

Finally edit your description for errors in grammar, usage, punctuation, and spelling. Invite a friend or your writing group to help you check for mistakes. Correct any errors and make a clean copy. You don't want carelessness to be part of your reputation as a reporter.

Publishing
YOUR EYEWITNESS DESCRIPTION

Before you send your manuscript to the local newspaper or school magazine or share it with your family, make another copy for your records (in case an editor has questions, or the original copy gets lost). To share your report orally, read it to your class, your friends or family, the hero, or any person or group who might be inspired by it.

If you have photographs of the heroic event, include them with your report for visual interest. They'll also remind your audience that your hero or heroine is real, like them.

A Heroic Effort

by Michelle Parisi

St. Charles, Illinois

I never thought Maria was heroic in any way until Kevin arrived at school. At first I didn't pay any attention to Kevin either—he was always so silent and solitary, sitting at the back of the room. For some reason, no one wanted him in their group, and nobody tried to make friends with him.

Even though Maria and I hung out with a group of our own, something about the new boy's independence touched us. Maria in particular sensed his loneliness every time she looked at him. We didn't like the way kids called him "the loser" and attacked him because of his independence.

Maria was repulsed by this lack of respect for others, but what she found even more horrible was the lack of respect these people had for themselves. Kevin seemed to be the only one who had any real backbone and sense of self-worth, and this inspired us to become his friends.

One day, Maria and I scoured the lunch room for Kevin and discovered him in a secluded corner. I went with her as she squeezed through the packed room and plunked herself across from him. She placed her lunch on the table, hesitated slightly, and said "Hello."

Conversation was a bit slow at first, as we all three picked at our food uneasily. But soon enough, we warmed up to each other like old friends.

The next day Maria spotted Kevin in the cafeteria and waved, but as she walked toward him, she was stopped dead in her tracks. There seemed to be a human roadblock, formed for her inconvenience. She hardly recognized the people she had once called her friends. Instead of teenagers, they now looked more like a wolf pack in search of prey to rip to shreds. They resembled that same pack in another way—they were too cowardly to confront a creature alone.

To the mob's surprise, Maria solidly stood her ground. I stood a little behind her, to observe the situation.

"So you're hangin' out with the loser, huh?" Snickers traveled through the group like an electric current. The wolves licked their lips, anticipating and closing in for the kill. They awaited response from their victim.

"He's not a loser," Maria said, straining with the effort to keep her voice level. "He's my friend."

The pack was confused. Was she actually standing up to them—by herself? Then from the pack the voice spoke again, but this time more softly. "Why would you hang out with that loser if you could hang out with us?"

Maria's words came out in an angry explosion. "I don't even know who you guys are. You cover up your real identity because you're afraid people will laugh at the things that make each one of you different. That makes you the losers! Now if you'll excuse me." Maria shoved through the stunned crowd and joined her new friend.

I learned a lot about heroism that day. I saw how courage can come in many shapes and forms. And most of all, I learned that the secret to being a hero is simply helping someone in need.

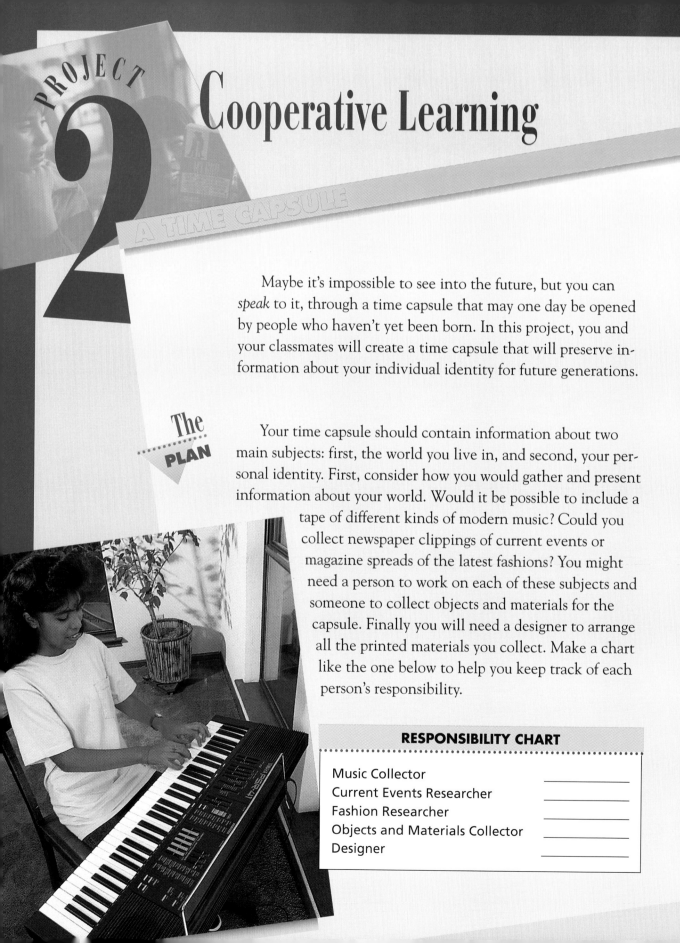

Cooperative Learning

PROJECT 2

A TIME CAPSULE

Maybe it's impossible to see into the future, but you can *speak* to it, through a time capsule that may one day be opened by people who haven't yet been born. In this project, you and your classmates will create a time capsule that will preserve information about your individual identity for future generations.

The PLAN

Your time capsule should contain information about two main subjects: first, the world you live in, and second, your personal identity. First, consider how you would gather and present information about your world. Would it be possible to include a tape of different kinds of modern music? Could you collect newspaper clippings of current events or magazine spreads of the latest fashions? You might need a person to work on each of these subjects and someone to collect objects and materials for the capsule. Finally you will need a designer to arrange all the printed materials you collect. Make a chart like the one below to help you keep track of each person's responsibility.

RESPONSIBILITY CHART

Music Collector	_____
Current Events Researcher	_____
Fashion Researcher	_____
Objects and Materials Collector	_____
Designer	_____

The PERSONAL INFORMATION

Now work on the personal information you'd like to include. Write a short introduction, giving your date of birth and a brief physical description. Then describe the kind of person you are. Think about your strengths and abilities. Do you have **physical** skills that you communicate through physical activities such as sports, dance, or charades? Do you have **musical** talents that help you in activities such as rap, choral reading, composing, and singing? Perhaps you have a strong **visual** sense, with a knack for copying, designing, sculpting, or repairing things, or **interpersonal** skills that give you the ability to cooperate, negotiate, empathize, or interact with others. Whatever your strengths, make sure you define them in your description of yourself. When you have finished your description, add it to the time capsule.

The PRODUCT

Now that you've gathered all the information that you'd like to preserve, discuss what to use as a time capsule and where to put it. Could you use a tin box or a plastic container? Should you bury it or send it to your local archives or museum? Think of a place that will safely preserve your identity for future generations.

Helping Your Community

BECOME AN INSPIRATION

A work of art not only expresses the individuality of its creator, but inspires others to create as well. In this project, you'll use your creativity to produce a work of art that expresses who you've become. Then, with a small group or your entire class, you'll decide how to present your work in a way that encourages others to express themselves, too.

Creating SOMETHING UNIQUE

Base the choice for your work of art on your talents. Are you a good musician? Then write a song! Do you like to paint? Create a self-portrait! Make a collage or a jigsaw puzzle, or construct a mobile of your childhood memories. Express yourself through dance or sculpture if you prefer. Create something that represents some aspect of your individuality—a work of art that will inspire others.

To help you think of things to express about yourself, try jotting down answers to questions like the ones below. Then brainstorm a list of the things that each question brings to mind—such as colors, tunes, places, events, pictures, or faces. Try to incorporate some of these into your creation.

- How do I see myself?
- What sort of things do I like?
- How did I get to be who I am?
- Does my identity remain the same, or do I change at different times and in different places?

Presenting YOUR WORK

Once you've completed your work of art, hold a small group or class meeting to decide where to present your work. Consider a homeless shelter, a hospice, a home for physically handicapped young people, a retirement community, or the pediatric unit of a hospital. Then contact the organization to see if it would like to provide a space for your presentation.

Use your presentation as an opportunity to encourage others to create something. Present a talk, a video tape, or a written explanation of your creative process. Show others how to ask the questions that you've asked yourself. Help them locate their own talents and hidden strengths. Include an introduction explaining the value of understanding the qualities that make each person unique.

Putting It All Together

What Have You Learned About the Theme?

Now that you've finished *Becoming Myself*, think about how your attitudes toward this theme and your own identity have changed. Look back at the writing you've done for this unit—in your journal, in response to your reading, in the Writing Workshop. Show what you have learned about this theme by writing an encyclopedia entry about yourself.

AN ENTRY OF YOUR OWN

Prewriting and Drafting   First, find an encyclopedia entry of someone famous, just to get an idea of how to write one about yourself. Notice that the entry gives information about the person's life and achievements. When you have finished studying the encyclopedia entry, make a web about what makes you who you are. Include your special qualities, the people and events that have especially influenced you, and the literature and activities in this unit that have most strongly affected you.

Begin your entry by giving information about your early life, such as where you were born, lived, and went to school.

Remember to refer to yourself in the third person, using the pronoun *he* or *she*. Then write about your interests and your special qualities and achievements. If you like, describe something that you will do in the future because of your special qualities; imagine what achievement might be listed in a future encyclopedia. Think of several possibilities and then pick one.

Revising and Editing   Exchange entries with a partner or writing group. Ask for comments on and advice about the content of your writing. Try making a few different drafts until you have one that pleases you. Finally, have your partner or writing group check for errors in grammar, spelling, and punctuation.

Publishing   Write your encyclopedia entry neatly and give it a title. Post it on a class bulletin board so that your classmates can read it or add it to your classmates' entries, arranging the entries alphabetically.

Evaluating Your Work

In a small group, discuss the Big Questions on pages 10-11. In your journal, comment on how your responses have changed following your work in this unit.

Think Back About Your Work

Now think about the unit you've just finished and evaluate your work, including your reading, your writing, your activities, and your projects. Be realistic and honest about your progress, but don't be too hard on yourself.

Write a note to your teacher explaining what you've accomplished during this unit. Use the following questions to help you write your note.

- How have your ideas about becoming yourself changed? What literature selections or activities in this unit helped to bring about this change?

- Which literature selections that you read in this unit did you enjoy most and least? Why?

- What did you learn as you worked on your project? What would you do differently if you worked on a similar project again?

- What suggestions would you make to your teacher about presenting this unit next time?

- How do you rate your work in this unit? Use the following scale and explain why you chose this number.

  1 = Outstanding   3 = Fair
  2 = Good   4 = Not as good as it could have been

POINT OF VIEW

What Is Point of View?

Point of view is the way a story is told. Sometimes a *narrator*, or speaker, tells the story from a personal point of view, referring to himself or herself using pronouns like *I, we, our* and *us*. This is called *first-person point of view*. For example, in the literature selection "Who Am I?" the speaker describes the world from a very personal point of view: "I walk through crowded streets. . . ." In *third-person point of view*, on the other hand, the narrator stands back from the action and describes what happens to others. A third-person narrator may be *omniscient* (all-knowing) or *limited* (taking the point of view of a particular character).

Rewriting a Story Look through the literature selections you've read for a character whose point of view was never revealed, such as the dragon in "Young Ladies Don't Slay Dragons" or one of the boys in "Through the Tunnel." Then retell the story from the first-person point of view using that character's voice. Describe what you think about the other characters and how you feel about the events of the story.

Write About Your Life Think of an important event in your life that you can remember clearly, such as your first day in a new school. Now step back from the event and write a short story about it from the third-person omniscient point of view. Remember that in this kind of narrative you must use the pronoun *he* or *she* when referring to yourself.

What Is Conflict?

Conflict is the struggle that a character must face in a work of literature. The conflict can be *external*—as in one character against another, one character against nature, or one character against society—or it can be *internal*—taking place inside the character's mind. Conflict is important to the story's plot and helps reveal a character's identity. In the literature selection from *I Know Why the Caged Bird Sings*, the narrator struggles to become the first African American to work on the San Francisco streetcars. Her victory reveals not only her strength of character but also the importance of conflict in both literature and life.

Write a Diary   Look through the literature selections you've read for a character facing a special conflict. This conflict could be internal or external. Then imagine you are that character and write a series of diary entries that parallel the action of the story. Describe how you feel about the story's events and tell what you hope to gain from the conflict.

Turning Reality into Fiction   The world is full of the raw material of stories. Look through a newspaper or magazine for examples of real-life conflict. The conflict could be between one person and another; it might also be between one person and society or nature. Choose an article about a person who is experiencing some kind of conflict. Then write a story about the conflict. Include dialogue and description.

GLOSSARY OF LITERARY TERMS

A

alliteration Repetition of the first sound—usually a consonant sound—in several words of a sentence or a line of poetry.

allusion An author's indirect reference to someone or something that is presumed to be familiar to the reader.

anecdote A short narrative about an interesting or a humorous event, usually in the life of a person.

antagonist The person or force opposing the protagonist, or main character in a literary work. [See also *protagonist*.]

autobiography A person's written account of his or her own life.

B

ballad A poem, often a song, that tells a story in simple verse.

biography An account of a person's life, written by another person.

blank verse Unrhymed poetry.

C

character A person or an animal that participates in the action of a work of literature. A *dynamic character* is one whose thoughts, feelings, and actions are changeable and lifelike; a *static character* always remains the same. [See also *protagonist, antagonist*.]

characterization The creation of characters through the characters' use of language and through descriptions of their appearance, thoughts, emotions, and actions. [See also *character*.]

chronology An arrangement of events in the order in which they happen.

cliché An overused expression that is trite rather than meaningful.

climax The highest point of tension in the plot of a work of literature. [See also *plot*.]

comedy An amusing play that has a happy ending.

conclusion The final part or ending of a piece of literature.

concrete poem A poem arranged on the page so that its punctuation, letters, and lines make the shape of the subject of the poem.

conflict A problem that confronts the characters in a piece of literature. The conflict may be *internal* (a character's struggle within himself or herself) or *external* (a character's struggle against nature, another person, or society). [See also *plot*.]

context The general sense of words that helps readers to understand the meaning of unfamiliar words and phrases in a piece of writing.

D

description An author's use of words to give the reader or listener a mental picture, an impression, or an understanding of a person, place, thing, event, or idea.

dialect A form of speech spoken by people in a particular group or geographical region that differs in vocabulary, grammar, and pronunciation from the standard language.

dialogue The spoken words and conversation of characters in a work of literature.

drama A play that is performed before an audience according to stage directions and using dialogue. Classical drama has two genres: *tragedy* and *comedy*. Modern drama includes *melodrama, satire, theater of the absurd*, and *pantomime*. [See also *comedy, play*, and *tragedy*.]

dramatic poetry A play written in the form of poetry.

E

epic A long narrative poem—written in a formal style and meant to be read aloud—that relates the adventures and experiences of one or more great heroes or heroines.

essay   Personal nonfiction writing about a particular subject that is important to the writer.

excerpt   A passage from a larger work that has been taken out of its context to be used for a special purpose.

exposition   Writing that explains, analyzes, or defines.

extended metaphor   An elaborately drawn out metaphor. [See also *metaphor*.]

F

fable   A short, simple story whose purpose is to teach a lesson, usually with animal characters who talk and act like people.

fantasy   Imaginative fiction about unrealistic characters, places, and events.

fiction   Literature, including the short story and the novel, that tells about imaginary people and events.

figurative language
Language used to express ideas through figures of speech: descriptions that aren't meant to be taken literally. Types of figurative language include *simile*, *metaphor*, *extended metaphor*, *hyperbole*, and *personification*.

figure of speech   A type of figurative language, not meant to be taken literally, that expresses something in such a way that it brings the thing to life in the reader's or listener's imagination. [See also *figurative language*.]

flashback   A break in a story's action that relates a past happening in order to give the reader background information about a present action in the story.

folktale   A story that has been passed along from storyteller to storyteller for generations. Kinds of folktales include *tall tales*, *fairy tales*, *fables*, *legends*, and *myths*.

foreshadowing   The use of clues to create suspense by giving the reader or audience hints of events to come.

free verse   Poetry that has no formal rhyme scheme or metrical pattern.

G

genre   A major category of art. The three major literary genres are poetry, prose, and drama.

H

haiku   A three-line Japanese verse form. In most haiku, the first and third lines have five syllables, while the second line has seven. The

traditional haiku describes a complicated feeling or thought in simple language through a single image.

hero/heroine   The main character in a work of literature. In heroic literature, the hero or heroine is a particularly brave, noble, or clever person whose achievements are unusual and important. [See also *character*.]

heroic age   The historical period in western civilization—from about 800 B.C. through A.D. 200—during which most works of heroic literature, such as myths and epics, were created in ancient Greece and Rome.

hubris   Arrogance or excessive pride leading to mistakes; the character flaw in a hero of classical tragedy.

hyperbole   An obvious exaggeration used for emphasis. [See also *figurative language*.]

I

idiom   An expression whose meaning cannot be understood from the ordinary meaning of the words. For example, *It's raining cats and dogs*.

imagery   The words and phrases in writing that appeal to the senses of sight, hearing, taste, touch, and smell.

irony   An effect created by a sharp contrast between what is expected and what is real. An *ironic twist* in a plot is an event that is the complete opposite of what the characters have been hoping or expecting will happen. An *ironic statement* declares the opposite of the speaker's literal meaning.

J

jargon   Words and phrases used by a group of people who share the same profession or special interests in order to refer to technical things or processes with which they are familiar. In general, jargon is any terminology that sounds unclear, overused, or pretentious.

L

legend   A famous folktale about heroic actions, passed along by word of mouth from generation to generation. The legend may have begun as a factual account of real people and events but has become mostly or completely fictitious.

limerick   A form of light verse, or humorous poetry, written in one five-line stanza with a regular scheme of rhyme and meter.

literature   The branch of art that is expressed in written language and includes all written genres.

lyric poem   A short poem that expresses personal feelings and thoughts in a musical way. Originally, lyrics were the words of songs that were sung to music played on the lyre, a stringed instrument invented by the ancient Greeks.

M

metamorphosis   The transformation of one thing, or being, into another completely different thing or being, such as a caterpillar's change into a butterfly.

metaphor   Figurative language in which one thing is said to be another thing. [See also *figurative language*.]

meter   The pattern of rhythm in lines of poetry. The most common meter, in poetry written in English, is iambic pentameter, that is, a verse having five metrical feet, each foot of verse having two syllables, an unaccented one followed by an accented one.

mood   The feeling or atmosphere that a reader senses while reading or listening to a work of literature.

motivation   A character's reasons for doing, thinking, feeling, or saying something. Sometimes an author will make a character's motivation obvious from the beginning. In realistic fiction and drama, however, a character's motivation may be so complicated that the reader discovers it gradually, by studying the character's thoughts, feelings, and behavior.

myth   A story, passed along by word of mouth for generations, about the actions of gods and goddesses or superhuman heroes and heroines. Most myths were first told to explain the origins of natural things or to justify the social rules and customs of a particular society.

N

narration   The process of telling a story. For both fiction and nonfiction, there are two main kinds of narration, based on whether the story is told from a first-person or third-person point of view. [See also *point of view*.]

narrative poem   A poem that tells a story containing the basic literary ingredients of fiction: character, setting, and plot.

narrator   The person, or voice, that tells a story. [See also *point of view, voice*.]

nonfiction   Prose that is factually true and is about real people, events, and places.

nonstandard English Versions of English, such as slang and dialects, that use pronunciation, vocabulary, idiomatic expressions, grammar, and punctuation that differ from the accepted "correct" constructions of English.

novel A long work of narrative prose fiction. A novel contains narration, a setting or settings, characters, dialogue, and a more complicated plot than a short story.

O

onomatopoeia The technique of using words that imitate the sounds they describe, such as *hiss*, *buzz*, and *splash*.

oral tradition Stories, poems, and songs that have been kept alive by being told, recited, and sung by people over many generations. Since the works were not originally written, they often have many different versions.

P

parable A brief story—similar to a fable, but about people—that describes an ordinary situation and concludes with a short moral or lesson to be learned.

personification Figurative language in which an animal, an object, or an idea is given human characteristics. [See also *figurative language*.]

persuasion A type of speech or writing whose purpose is to convince people that something is true or important.

play A work of dramatic literature written for performance by actors before an audience. In classical or traditional drama, a play is divided into five acts, each containing a number of scenes. Each act represents a distinct phase in the development of the plot. Modern plays often have only one act and one scene.

playwright The author of a play.

plot The sequence of actions and events in fiction or drama. A traditional plot has at least three parts: the *rising action*, leading up to a turning point that affects the main character; the *climax*, the turning point or moment of greatest intensity or interest; and the *falling action*, leading away from the conflict, or resolving it.

poetry Language selected and arranged in order to say something in a compressed or nonliteral way. Modern poetry may or may not use many of the traditional poetic techniques that include *meter*, *rhyme*, *alliteration*, *figurative language*, *symbolism*, and *specific verse forms*.

point of view The perspective from which a writer tells a story. *First-person* narrators tell the story from their own point of view, using pronouns such as *I* or *me*. *Third-person* narrators, using pronouns such as *he*, *she*, or *them*, may be *omniscient* (knowing everything about all characters), or *limited* (taking the point of view of one character). [See also *narration*.]

propaganda Information or ideas that may or may not be true, but are spread as though they are true, in order to persuade people to do or believe something.

prose The ordinary form of written and spoken language used to create fiction, nonfiction, and most drama.

protagonist The main character of a literary work. [See also *character* and *characterization*.]

R

refrain A line or group of lines that is repeated, usually at the end of each verse, in a poem or a song.

repetition The use of the same formal element more than once in a literary work, for emphasis or in order to achieve another desired effect.

resolution The falling action in fiction or drama,

including all of the developments that follow the climax and show that the story's conflict is over. [See also *plot*.]

rhyme scheme   A repeated pattern of similar sounds, usually found at the ends of lines of poetry or poetic drama.

rhythm   In poetry, the measured recurrence of accented and unaccented syllables in a particular pattern. [See also *meter*.]

S

scene   The time, place, and circumstances of a play or a story. In a play, a scene is a section of an act. [See also *play*.]

science fiction   Fantasy literature set in an imaginary future, with details and situations that are designed to seem scientifically possible.

setting   The time and place of a work of literature.

short story   Narrative prose fiction that is shorter and has a less complicated plot than a novel. A short story contains narration, at least one setting, at least one character, and usually some dialogue.

simile   Figurative language that compares two unlike things, introduced by the words "like" or "as." [See also *figurative language*.]

soliloquy   In a play, a short speech spoken by a single character when he or she is alone on the stage. A soliloquy usually expresses the character's innermost thoughts and feelings, when he or she thinks no other characters can hear.

sonnet   A poem written in one stanza, using fourteen lines of iambic pentameter. [See also *meter*.]

speaker   In poetry, the individual whose voice seems to be speaking the lines. [See also *narration*, *voice*.]

stage directions   The directions, written by the playwright, to tell the director, actors, and theater technicians how a play should be dramatized. Stage directions may specify such things as how the setting should appear in each scene, how the actors should deliver their lines, when the stage curtain should rise and fall, how stage lights should be used, where on the stage the actors should be during the action, and when sound effects should be used.

stanza   A group of lines in poetry set apart by blank lines before and after the group; a poetic verse.

style   The distinctive way in which an author composes a work of literature in written or spoken language.

suspense   An effect created by authors of various types of fiction and drama, especially adventure and mystery, to heighten interest in the story.

symbol   An image, person, place, or thing that is used to express the idea of something else.

T

tall tale   A kind of folk tale, or legend, that exaggerates the characteristics of its hero or heroine.

theme   The main idea or underlying subject of a work of literature.

tone   The attitude that a work of literature expresses to the reader through its style.

tragedy   In classical drama, a tragedy depicts a noble hero or heroine who makes a mistake of judgment that has disastrous consequences.

V

verse   A stanza in a poem. Also, a synonym for poetry as a genre. [See also *stanza*.]

voice   The narrator or the person who relates the action of a piece of literature. [See also *speaker*.]

ACKNOWLEDGMENTS

Grateful acknowledgment is made for permission to reprint the following copyrighted material.

"The Sun and the Moon" by Elaine Laron from *Free to Be...You and Me* by Marlo Thomas and Associates. Copyright © 1974 by Free to Be Foundation, Inc. Used by permission of Bantam Books, a division of Bantam Doubleday Dell Publishing Group, Inc.

"Who Am I?" by Stella Mancillas is reprinted from *I Heard a Scream in the Street : Poems by Young People in the City* selected by Nancy Larrick, copyright © 1970 by Nancy Larrick

"Young Ladies Don't Slay Dragons" by Joyce Hovelsrud is reprinted from *The Princess Book*, copyright © 1974 by Rand McNally & company. By permission of the author.

From *I Know Why the Caged Bird Sings* by Maya Angelou. Copyright © 1969 by Maya Angelou. Reprinted by permission of Random House, Inc.

"74th Street" from *The Malibu and Other Poems* by Myra Cohn Livingston. Copyright © 1972 by Myra Cohn Livingston (Atheneum). Reprinted by permission of Marian Reiner for the author.

from *The Olympic Games* by Theodore Knight. Reprinted by permission of Lucent Books, Inc., P.O. Box 289011, San Diego, CA 92198-9011.

"Through the Tunnel" from *The Habit of Loving* by Doris Lessing, copyright © 1957 by Doris Lessing. Originally appeared in *The New Yorker*. Reprinted by permission of HarperCollins Publishers.

"For Poets" by Al Young is reprinted from *The Song Turning Back Into Itself* by Al Young, copyright © 1965 by Al Young. By permission of the author.

"Raymond's Run" from *Gorilla, My Love* by Toni Cade Bambara. Copyright © 1971 by Toni Cade Bambara. Reprinted by permission of Random House.

"What a Boy Can Do" by Alberto Ríos is reprinted from *Teodoro Luna's Two Kisses*, Poems by Alberto Ríos, by permission of W.W. Norton & Company, Inc. Copyright © 1990 by Alberto Ríos.

"Thumbprint" from *It Doesn't Always Have to Rhyme* by Eve Merriam. Copyright © 1964 by Eve Merriam. © renewed 1992 by Eve Merriam. Reprinted by permission of Marian Reiner.

"Pictures on a Rock" from *To Live in Two Worlds: American Indian Youth Today* by Brent Ashabranner. Copyright © 1984 by Brent Ashabranner. Reprinted by permission of the author.

"On Shark's Tooth Beach" from *Throwing Shadows* by E. L. Konigsburg. Copyright ©1979 by E. L. Konigsburg. Reprinted with the permission of Atheneum Publishers, an imprint of Macmillan Publishing Company.

ILLUSTRATION

11 Heidi Lutts; 16-23 K. Boake W.

PHOTOGRAPHY

4 *l* Tony Freeman/PhotoEdit; *r* Jim Whitmer/Stock Boston; 5 Reproduced by the courtesy of the Trustees, The National Gallery, London; 6 Julie Bidwell/©D.C. Heath; 10 *t* Skjold/The Image Works; *b* John Owens/©D.C. Heath; 11 *t* Sarah Putnam/©D.C. Heath; *c* John Owens/©D.C. Heath; *b* Jim Whitmer/Stock Boston; 12 *inset* NASA; 12-13 *background* ©Jay Pasachoff; 13 *inset* Richard Hamilton Smith; 14-15 Art Gallery of Ontario, Toronto. Gift of Mr. and Mrs. Morris Emer, 1985. ©Helen Frankenthaler, 1993. Photo by Carlo Catenazzi; 24-25, 29 UPI/Bettmann; 29 *inset* Mary Ellen Mark Library; 32, 34-35 UPI/Bettmann; 35 *inset* AP/Wide World Photos; 36-37 Collection Mr. & Mrs. Albert Hackett, NY. ©Estate of Ben Shahn/VAGA, NY, 1995; 37 Courtesy of Holiday House; 38 Focus on Sports; *inset,* 41 UPI/Bettmann; 43 Dan Helms/Duomo; *inset* Anne Knight; 44-59 Clem Spalding; 59 *inset* Miriam Berkley; 60 Reproduced by courtesy of the Trustees, The National Gallery, London; 62-63, 64-65, 66-67 David Madison; 69 David Madison/Duomo; 70-71 David Madison; 72, 73 Focus on Sports; 73 *inset* Carole Dufrechou. Courtesy of Random House Group, Inc.; 74-75 *background* Dan Derdula; 75 *inset* Photo by Hal Martin Fogel. Courtesy of W.W. Norton and Company; 77 *inset* Courtesy of Macmillan Children's Book Group; 78-81 Lauren Shaw; 81 *t, inset* Paul Conklin; *b, inset* AP/Wide World Photos; 82-83 Richard Hamilton Smith; *insets* Sinclair Stammers/Photo Researchers; 86, 91 Kevin Altken/Peter Arnold; 92-93 Daniel Derdula; 93 *inset* Jeffrey Rotman/Peter Arnold; 94 Norbert Wu/Peter Arnold; 99 James Karales/Peter Arnold; 101 Richard Hamilton Smith; 101 *inset* Stu Perry. Courtesy of Macmillan Children's Book Group. **Back cover** *t* Julie Bidwell/©D.C. Heath; *c* Sarah Putnam/©D.C. Heath; *b* Julie Bidwell/©D.C. Heath.

Full Pronunciation Key for Footnoted Words

(Each pronunciation and definition is adapted from *Scott, Foresman Advanced Dictionary* by E.L. Thorndike and Clarence L. Barnhart.)

The pronunciation of each footnoted word is shown just after the word, in this way: **abbreviate** [ə brē′ vē āt]. The letters and signs used are pronounced as in the words below. The mark ′ is placed after a syllable with primary or heavy accent, as in the example above. The mark ′ after a syllable shows a secondary or lighter accent, as in **abbreviation** [ə brē′ vē ā′ shən].

Some words, taken from foreign languages, are spoken with sounds that do not otherwise occur in English. Symbols for these sounds are given in the key as "foreign sounds."

a	hat, cap	j	jam, enjoy	u	cup, butter	
ā	age, face	k	kind, seek	u̇	full, put	
ä	father, far	l	land, coal	ü	rule, move	
		m	me, am	v	very, save	
b	bad, rob	n	no, in	w	will, woman	
ch	child, much	ng	long, bring	y	young, yet	
d	did, red			z	zero, breeze	
		o	hot, rock	zh	measure, seizure	
e	let, best	ō	open, go			
ē	equal, be	ô	order, all	ə represents:	
ėr	term, learn	oi	oil, voice		a in about	
		ou	house, out		e in taken	
f	fat, if				i in pencil	
g	go, bag	p	paper, cup		o in lemon	
h	he, how	r	run, try		u in circus	
		s	say, yes			
i	it, pin	sh	she, rush			
ī	ice, five	t	tell, it			
		th	thin, both			
		ᵮH	then, smooth			

foreign sounds

Y as in French *du*. Pronounce (ē) with the lips rounded as for (ü).

à as in French *ami*. Pronounce (ä) with the lips spread and held tense.

œ as in French *peu*. Pronounce (ā) with the lips rounded as for (ō).

N as in French *bon*. The N is not pronounced, but shows that the vowel before it is nasal.

H as in German *ach*. Pronounce (k) without closing the breath passage.